The Essentials of Instrumentation

Percussion Exam   Monday March 30th

1) Terms - French/German/Italian → Tambourine, Vibraphone, Timpani, Tenor Drum, Suspended Cymbals

Cymbals, Glockenspiel, Snare, Xylophone, Chimes, Bass Drum, Tom Tom, Triangle

2) construct percussion part

3) Know pitch ranges for 4 timps
     spelled

ranges for: Celeste, Marimba
and if they
sound octave   glockenspiel → orchestrabells,
up or not
etc   chimes, xylophone

D0072535

The Essentials of Instrumentation

Brad Hansen

Ball State University

Mayfield Publishing Company
Mountain View, California
London • Toronto

Copyright © 1991 by Mayfield Publishing Company

All rights reserved. No portion of this book may be reproduced in
any form or by any means without written permission of the publisher.

Library of Congress Cataloging-in-Publication Data

Hansen, Brad.
     The essentials of instrumentation / Brad Hansen.
          p.   cm.
     Includes bibliographical references and index.
     ISBN 0–87484–986–1
     1. Instrumentation and orchestration.   I. Title.
MT70.H17   1990
784.13'7 — dc20   90–13282
                                               CIP
                                               MN

Manufactured in the United States of America
10 9 8 7 6 5 4

Mayfield Publishing Company
1240 Villa Street
Mountain View, California 94041

Sponsoring editor, Janet M. Beatty; managing editor, Linda Toy;
production editor, Sondra Glider; manuscript editor, Sylvia Stein Wright;
text and cover designer, Joan Greenfield; music compositor, A/R Editions.
The text was set in 10.5/12 Century Old Style by Thompson Type and
printed on 50# Finch Opaque by Bawden Printing.

The Bizet, Mozart, Rimsky-Korsakov, and Wolf musical excerpts are used with permission of Belwin
Mills Publishing Company. The scoring excerpt by Robert Ehle is used with permission of the composer.

Preface

After watching my students struggle with excessively detailed texts and separate workbooks of scoring exercises, I realized that they needed a straightforward, concise, and practical scoring text that was both effective and affordable. I decided to create, in a single volume, a book that combined the necessary information, creative exercises, scoring projects, and score excerpts that students need to learn the fundamentals of instrumentation and orchestration.

The Essentials of Instrumentation emphasizes the practical, traditional applications for instruments. After students have mastered this material, they will have the perspective to approach contemporary devices and create unusual effects with the use of extended instrumental techniques and new methods of notation.

Acoustics, conventions of notation, transposition, and score reduction are the primary subjects treated in Chapter One. Developing proper manuscript skills from the beginning gives students confidence and helps them take pride in their work. Chapter Two through Chapter Five cover families of instruments, including the orchestral strings, woodwinds, brass, and percussion. At the conclusion of each chapter are scoring exercises so that students can apply the information they have learned about the instruments. In Chapter Six chordal instruments are discussed, along with processes for developing an accompaniment. Chapter Seven addresses transcribing for orchestra, handling lines, textures, colors, and chords. Important background information is given in Chapter Eight on the historical development of instruments and the origins of orchestral style. By learning about the resources available to a composer, students can develop a perspective that allows them to assess orchestral style. Points to consider when analyzing orchestration conclude Chapter Eight.

The appendixes are an integral part of the text and central to its pedagogy. The glossary of foreign terms in Appendix A is an indispensable aid to the student in deciphering score directions. The anthology of orchestral excerpts included in Appendix B offers choice examples for study. A cassette recording of these excerpts is available to instructors using the book, so that students can hear as well as see a rich variety of scoring techniques. Developing a strong, clear aural imagination for instrument timbres, individually and in combination, is an important goal for orchestrators. Appendix C consists of scoring projects designed to be performed by students in the class. Solving problems of balance and projection with the instrumental resources at hand is the most practical approach, since ideal ensembles rarely exist. This practical experience is a key ingredient in the learning process.

An instructor's manual accompanies the text. It includes teaching strategies and possible solutions to creative projects and exercises; highlights points of interest regarding the orchestral excerpts found in Appendix B; and provides an extensive list of additional excerpts from the literature that illustrate the use of instruments individually and in combination.

ACKNOWLEDG-MENTS

I gratefully acknowledge all of my students for teaching me how to bring about learning. I would also like to thank the theory faculty at the University of Northern Colorado for their encouragement during my early years in teaching orchestration, especially Richard Bourassa, Evan Copley, Dale Dykins, and Robert Ehle. The applied faculty at Ball State University have graciously contributed their time, providing me with a better perspective on their instruments. I am indebted to Jan Beatty of Mayfield Publishing Company for her vision of the book and her good judgment, to Sondra Glider for her production skills, and to Sylvia Stein Wright for editing. Thanks also to the reviewers who played a key role in improving the book: George Ferencz, Idaho State University; George Heussenstamm, California State University, Los Angeles; Lathon Jernigan, University of Northern Iowa; George Longazo, California State University, Chico; Randall Shinn, Arizona State University; and Gary Smart, University of Wyoming. Deepest gratitude goes to my wife, Jani, for her help and support in all ways.

Contents

Chapter Six   81
Other Instruments

Chapter Seven   87
Scoring for the Orchestra

Chapter Eight   97
Orchestral Styles

Appendix C
Scoring Projects 169

The Essentials of Instrumentation

Chapter One

Sounds, Sources, and Symbols

The process of making musical tones consists of producing regular vibrations in the air at an audible level. These vibrations may be caused by a string and a resonator, by a column of air, or by any object that vibrates at a given frequency. The fundamental waveform of a vibrating system, its slowest possible rate of vibration, is governed by the length and dimensions of the system. Dividing the length of a vibrating string in half produces a pitch one octave higher than the full length of the string. One-third of the length produces a pitch an octave plus a perfect fifth higher, and one-fourth of the original length produces a pitch two octaves higher. The first four vibrational nodes of a string fastened at both ends are shown in the diagram below.

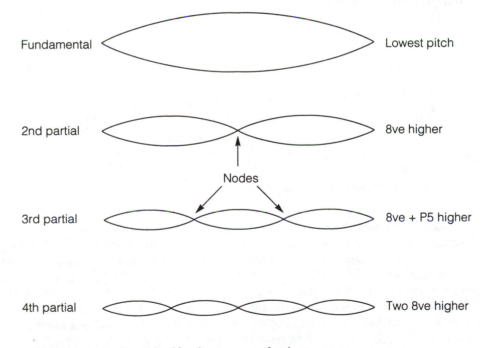

FIGURE 1.1   *Fundamental and first three overtones of a vibrating string*

Waves of pressure in a vibrating column of air act in much the same fashion as the vibrating string. The nodes are points of greater pressure within the column.

The composite waveform of any system is a combination of the fundamental and its multiples, or partials. In 1862 Hermann von Helmholtz demonstrated that the relative strength of the partials helps determine the tone color, or timbre, of a sound. It has since been proven that the attack, sustain, decay, and release of a sound over time are prime factors in recognizing a sound source. Formant regions, or frequencies where certain harmonics are more pronounced, are also important factors in identifying sounds.

A pipe that is open at both ends acts differently than one closed at one end, or stopped. Both are similarly affected by holes drilled in the sides, which relieve the pressure at a length that determines the pitch of a tone. The resonance curve for strings and open pipes is shown below, with the first nine partials present in decreasing strength.

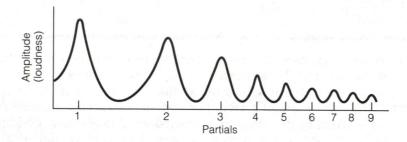

FIGURE 1.2   *Resonance curve of strings and open pipes*

The resonance curve for a pipe closed at one end is shown below, with the odd partials much stronger.

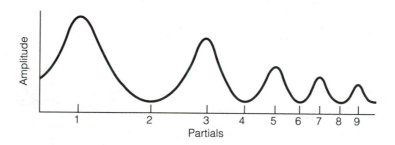

FIGURE 1.3   *Resonance curve of a stopped pipe*

Each of the partials of a vibrating system can be identified as a pitch in the overtone series. Knowledge of this series is relevant to understanding how most instruments function, particularly brass and strings. It is easy to remember the pitches in this harmonic series if they are related to the fundamental pitch as scale degrees in a major key. The second partial is an octave above the first partial, which is the fundamental or tonic. The third partial is a fifth in the major scale, the fourth partial another tonic, and the fifth partial is a third in the major scale. To find the scale degree from the ninth to the sixteenth partial, subtract seven from the number of the partial. For example, the thirteenth partial is the sixth scale degree.

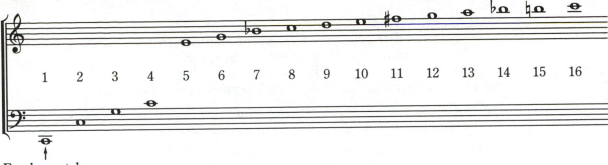

Fundamental

FIGURE 1.4 *Overtone series*

In the sixth century B. C., the Greek scholar Pythagoras observed that if a string were divided in half, the sound of half the string was an octave above the original fundamental pitch. He converted this information into a mathematical ratio between the frequency of the partial compared to the fundamental and went on to provide a mathematical ratio for each interval, as shown below.

Perfect octave	—	2:1
Perfect fifth	—	3:2
Perfect fourth	—	4:3
Major third	—	5:4
Major sixth	—	5:3
Minor third	—	6:5
Minor sixth	—	8:5
Minor seventh	—	9:5
Major seventh	—	15:8

Pythagorean tuning refers to the use of the 3:2 ratio for perfect fifths to determine the frequency of pitches in the scale. Because tuning in this method is not consistent with the pitches found in the overtone series, it is not used currently. Just tuning, which amounts to tuning perfect fourths and fifths and then the thirds above them, provides only three major triads in tune with the overtone series. These are the tonic, subdominant, and dominant chords in the key to which the instrument is tuned. Mean-tone tuning, a form of tempered just tuning, puts the thirds in tune and the fifths out of tune with the series. Equal temperament consists of twelve equal divisions, or semitones, to the octave. It is practical for keyboard instruments, but compared to the harmonic series, the seventh, eleventh, thirteenth, and fourteenth partials are quite out of tune. Equal temperament has become the accepted compromise for modulatory music involving keyboard and mallet instruments.

Chordophones—stringed instruments
   Lutes: violin, viola, cello, bass, guitar
   Zithers: harpsichord (psaltery), piano (dulcimer), clavichord
   Harps: harp (plane of strings is perpendicular to soundboard)

CLASSIFICATION OF INSTRUMENTS

Aerophones—wind instruments
   Lip vibrated: trumpet, horn, trombone, euphonium, tuba, all brass
   Flutes: transverse or vertical, whistle flute, recorder
   Reeds: Single—clarinet, saxophone
      Double—oboe, bassoon, English horn

Idiophones—struck instruments of solid design
   Triangle, cymbals, gong, bells, xylophone, vibraphone

Membranophones—stretched membrane
   Drums: timpani, tubular, frame (snare, field, tom-tom)

It is convenient for orchestrators to group instruments by section. The principal sections found in the orchestra are the woodwinds, brass, percussion, and strings. Voices and electronic sounds are commonly combined with acoustic instrument families, but they are beyond the scope of this text.

ORDER OF INSTRUMENTS

As a general rule, the instruments in each section are listed in the score from highest to lowest in pitch, top to bottom. They are ordered as follows, with typical numbers of each in an orchestra of moderate size. An asterisk (*) indicates that it is likely to be a double by a player of that instrument family. For example, if there were an English horn part, it would be performed by the second oboe player. If this part were added to two existing oboe parts, a third player would be required. The staff of a professional orchestra includes a player pool large enough to accommodate the needs of expansive scores, such as the tone poems by Richard Strauss.

ORCHESTRAL ORDER
WOODWINDS

Picc.	piccolo	1*
Fl.	flute	2
Ob.	oboe	2
E. Hn.	English horn	1*
Cl.	clarinet	2
B. Cl.	bass clarinet	1*
Bn.	bassoon	2
C. Bn.	contra bassoon	1*

BRASS

F Hn.	horn in F	4
Tpt.	trumpet	3
Trb.	trombone	3
Tuba	tuba	1

PERCUSSION

Timp.	timpani	1
Perc.	percussion	2–4
	nonpitched (drums, cymbal, triangle, tambourine)	
	pitched (xylophone, orchestra bells, chimes)	
Others	piano (Pno.), harp, celesta, organ, voices,	
	all others, including solo instrument in a concerto	

STRINGS

Vln. I	violin I	12–14
Vln. II	violin II	10–12
Vla.	viola	8–10
Vcl.	violoncello	6–8
Db.	double bass	4–6

It is important to memorize this score order because many publishers do not print the names or even the abbreviations for instruments after the first page of a score. This can become confusing if instruments not used on subsequent pages are deleted from the score. The order, clef, and transposition are the only clues the conductor has at times to determine which instruments are playing.

CHAMBER QUINTET ORDER

Mixed chamber groups usually follow the same order, omitting instruments not used. The order for standard chamber wind quintets is as follows:

Brass Quintet	*Woodwind Quintet*
Trumpet I	Flute
Trumpet II	Oboe
Horn	Clarinet
Trombone	Horn
Tuba	Bassoon

(handwritten annotations: "b FBEADG", "# GDAEBF", "from top", "from bottom"; beside brass quintet: "m2", "m2", "P5")

SCORE LAYOUT

The first page of music contains the title at the top, centered. In the upper right corner the composer's (and/or arranger's) names are given, and in the upper left corner it is wise to indicate whether the score is transposed for the instruments or in the concert key. The transposed score, showing each instrument's pitches as they appear in the parts, is highly recommended. The first line of music is indented slightly, with a double bar, and names of all instruments employed in the piece are spelled out in full. A bracket connects multiple staves for like instruments, such as first and second violins. In the score, bar lines will only connect sections and will be broken between woodwinds, brass, percussion, and strings.

Tempo markings are placed at the beginning of the music above the staff and often added above each section of the orchestra. Dynamic markings are placed below each individual part. Rehearsal letters or numbers are placed at convenient intervals throughout the score, typically at the top of each section. All notes and rests are aligned vertically with all other notes or rests that occur at the same time.

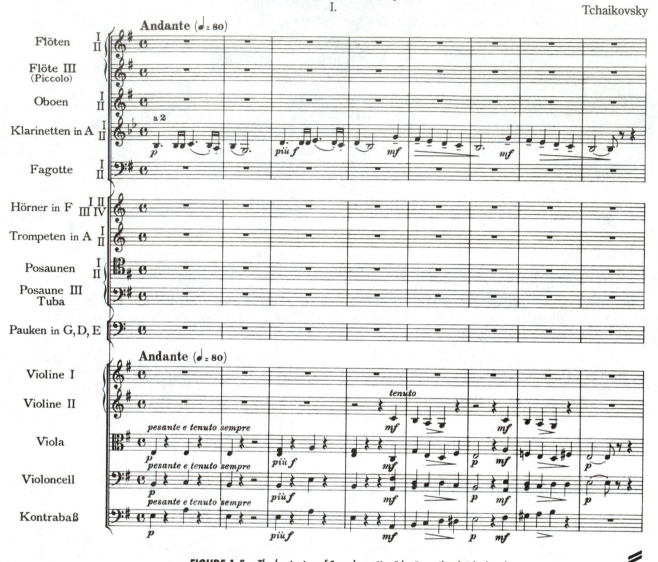

Fifth Symphony in E Minor, Op. 64
I.
Tchaikovsky

FIGURE 1.5 *The beginning of Symphony No. 5 by Peter Ilyitch Tchaikovsky*

THE PARTS

A separate copy of each instrumental part found in the score should be extracted for each performer. The first page contains the title of the piece centered, the composer's name at the upper right, and the name of the instrument that plays the part at the upper left. Following pages contain the name of the instrument (and part number if it applies), along with a page number. The first staff is indented, and the meter signature appears only at the beginning and at points of change. A clef and key signature are required on every staff. Rehearsal letters as they appear in the score are required, and cues should be indicated after lengthy periods of rest. A cue is written with small notes in the key and range of the instrumental part in which they appear. The original instrument's name is written above this brief passage, or cue, which occurs a few measures before the entry of the instrument for which the part is written. Rests of two or more consecutive measures are indicated by a solid line in the center of a measure, a multiple rest with the number of measures indicated above. Multiple rests should be divided for rehearsal letters, and an individual rest should be shown with a fermata in all parts if any instrument in the score has a fermata.

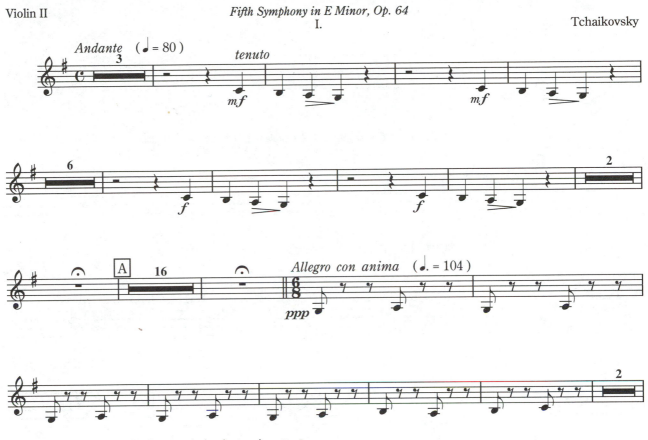

FIGURE 1.6   *Second violin part: Tchaikovsky, Symphony No. 5*

The word "tacet," meaning silent, is used when the performer does not play for an entire movement or, having completed the part, remains silent for the remainder of the piece. In a part where page turns must be made rapidly, v.s. (volte subito) is indicated at the bottom of the page. Measures of rest will ideally be placed before the page turns.

It is a great asset to the orchestrator to present performers with proper music manuscript. To do so, one must learn the shape of symbols in their conventional form. Students should constantly strive to improve the level of quality in their manuscript. A note head is an oval shape angled upwards to the right, not a slash or a round circle. A stem is three spaces or one octave in length. The exception to this rule is that if the note is two or more ledger lines away from the staff, the stem is extended to the middle line of that staff. Guidelines and examples illustrating correct manuscript are provided here for reference.

CONVENTIONS OF NOTATION

(a)

(b)

(c)

(d)

FIGURE 1.7 *How to draw (a) treble, (b) bass, (c) alto, and (d) tenor clefs*

FIGURE 1.8 *How to draw accidentals*

(a)

(b)

(c)

(d)

FIGURE 1.9 *Key signatures in (a) treble, (b) bass, (c) alto, and (d) tenor clefs*

FIGURE 1.10 *How to draw rests*

Notice the shape of the quarter rest, which most copyists draw from the bottom upwards. The horizontal part of the eighth rest lies in the third space, and all dots following rests of any value are also placed in the third space. Multiple measures of rest in a part are indicated by a thick horizontal line on the third space of the measure with thin vertical lines on both ends. A large numeral showing the number of measures of rest is placed above the staff.

FIGURE 1.11   *Chords with seconds and accidentals*

The note farthest from the center of the staff determines the stem direction of a chord. Draw the note heads first; then connect them with a stem that extends at least two lines past the last note of the chord. When drawing chords with the interval of a second, follow these steps:

1.   Determine the note farthest from the center of the staff, and write it.

2.   Add the stem in the proper direction.

3.   Moving away from the first written note, place the other notes along the stem on the correct side if possible.

The upper note will be placed on the right-hand side of the stem when the interval of a second occurs. The accidentals are added from top to bottom, moving from right to left, so that the top accidental is closest to the chord. If altered notes are placed along the stem at the interval of a seventh apart, then accidentals may be aligned vertically.

FIGURE 1.12   *Beamed units and borrowed groupings*

When a group of notes is to be beamed, the note farthest from the center of the staff determines whether the beam will be placed above or below the grouping. Beams follow the general contour of the notes, connecting the stems of the first and last notes of the grouping. If notes are more than one ledger line from the staff, the beam connecting them rests on the third line of the staff. All notes within a rhythmic unit, or metrical beat, should be beamed. However, beams may not extend between unit beat groupings. If there are rests within a group, do not extend multiple beams above or below the rest.

Borrowed groups, such as the triplet in 4/4 time, are designated by a number in the center of a bracket drawn over the note heads or the beam.

FIGURE 1.13 *Vertical alignment of two parts*

Exercise extreme care in aligning all beats in all parts of a score. This is probably the single most important factor affecting the ease with which a score can be interpreted.

FIGURE 1.14 *Placement of slurs*

Slurs ordinarily extend smoothly between note heads. They are placed outside staccato dots or tenuto dashes and inside percussive or pressure accents. A legato slur is generally placed over notes with stems pointing both up and down. If the last two notes under a slur are tied, extend the slur to the second note. When slurring two notes with different stem directions, slur over the top from note head to note head.

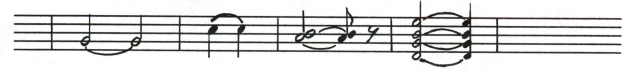

FIGURE 1.15 *Placement of ties*

Ties connect note heads of the same pitch. Notes above the center of the staff have ties curved above, and notes below the center have ties curved below.

FIGURE 1.16 *Two parts sharing a staff*

When two independent parts share a staff, seconds are written in reverse order, unless the voices cross, to give better stem placement. Slurs, articulations, and dynamics always appear nearest the part to which they apply.

One system of designating octaves is used consistently in this text. A simple way to remember it is to think of middle c as one line c. It is notated as c^1. The octave below is c; the octave above c^1 is c^2. All notes in the octave above each c have the same superscript numeric designation.

OCTAVE TERMINOLOGY

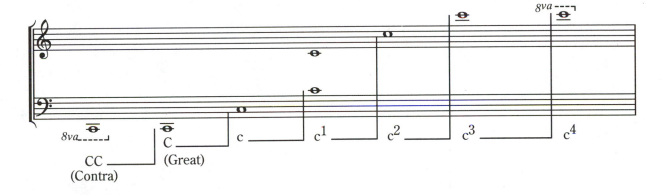

FIGURE 1.17 *Octave terminology*

The symbol "8va" is placed over a note or a passage that is to be played one octave higher, with a dotted line extending for the duration of the passage. The same designation is placed under a passage to be played an octave lower. The symbol "15ma" is used to indicate the distance of two octaves above or below the written pitch.

TRANSPOSITION

Most transposing instruments sound lower than written. The name of the instrument indicates the note that will sound when a written C is played. On a B♭ clarinet or trumpet the written pitch C produces a sound one step lower, the B♭. The practice in tonal music is to write the transposed part for a B♭ instrument in the key signature one step higher. For example, if the concert key (sounding pitch) of a composition is F, write the part in the key of G for a B♭ instrument.

When playing the written pitch C, a horn in F produces the sounding pitch F, a perfect fifth below the C. If the concert key of the music is E major, write the horn part in B major. When playing the written pitch C, a clarinet in A produces the sounding pitch A, a minor third below the C. If the music were in the concert key of D, the clarinet in A part would be transposed up to the key of F.

Scores written in the eighteenth and nineteenth centuries commonly contain parts written for natural horns and trumpets in various keys. In most cases the parts for these instruments without valves were written in the key of C, and the sounding pitch was below the written part. Thus, a horn in E♭ would sound a major sixth below the written pitch. Conversely, trumpets pitched in F, E, E♭, and D sound higher than written; those pitched in B, B♭, or A sound lower than written.

All ranges given for instruments in this text are written ranges, after transposition. Remember that you must TRANSPOSE UP from the concert pitch to the written pitch in almost all cases. The best way to transpose without errors is to think of the notes as scale degrees in the new key. For example, if a tonic triad is outlined in the concert key, a tonic triad must also be outlined in the transposed key. The following chart shows the interval and direction of transposition for some common wind instruments. A practical concert range is shown for reference.

Conservative Ranges

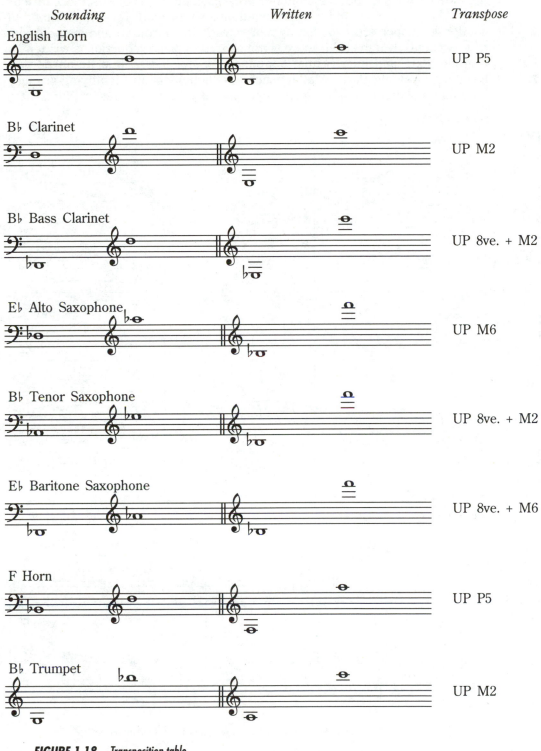

FIGURE 1.18 Transposition table

REDUCED SCORES

A condensed score shows the pitches present in the full score on three or four staves. Each choir might be represented on a single staff. It is often helpful to condense an open score to identify more clearly the harmonic and melodic content, particularly if the open score is transposed. A piano reduction is written on a grand staff, and nonessential doublings are deleted so that it can be performed by a single player. Making such a reduction entails identifying primary lines and moving the pitches from their transposed state to concert pitch.

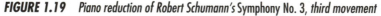

FIGURE 1.19 *Piano reduction of Robert Schumann's Symphony No. 3, third movement*

EXERCISES FOR PRACTICE

1. Write the two parts shown below with proper vertical alignment, at the
   sounding pitch for each.

2. Combine the parts for oboe 1 and oboe 2 on a single staff.

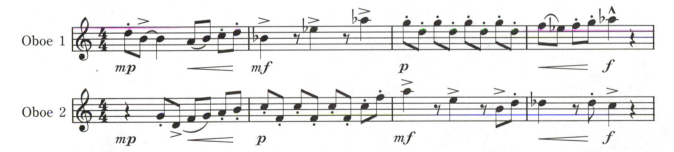

3. Create a piano reduction below of this excerpt from Brahms's *Variations on a Theme by Haydn*, Op. 56a.

4. Condense the excerpt from Haydn's Symphony No. 103 on the staves below.

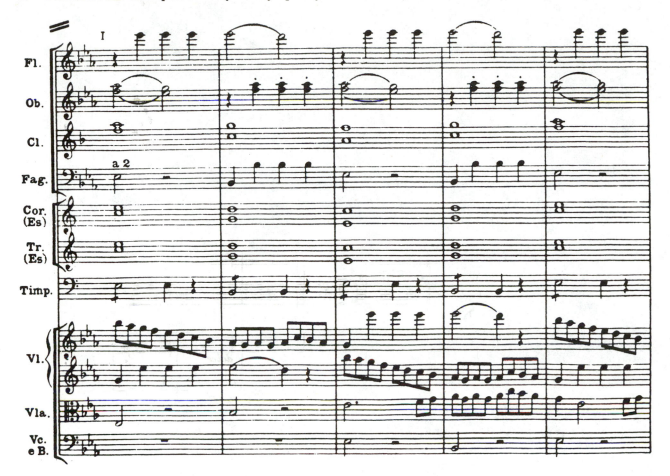

Chapter Two

Orchestral String Instruments

The string section is the largest group of similar instruments in the orchestra and for many reasons the most frequently employed. First and second violins form two separate sections, which can be compared to soprano voices in range. The violas provide alto or tenor range voices, and the cello section typically covers lines in the tenor and bass regions. Any of these instruments can be used in their upper range, becoming a more prominent voice in the texture. The double basses are a true bass voice for the section, sounding an octave below their written pitch. Some of the features of the strings that have made them the mainstay of the orchestra are listed below:

1. Strings are able to play continuously for long periods and can produce a sustained tone.
2. They have an enormous range of dynamic possibilities, from a whisper to a vibrant, full fortissimo.
3. The range in pitch they cover as a section is among the widest in the orchestra.
4. Virtually all types of technical maneuvers are effectively produced: fast passages, slow cantabile melodies, short or long tones, trills, tremolos, and chords.
5. Because of the vibrato, blend, and warmth of colors, strings do not tire the ear.

Vibrato: A normal part of the string sound. Although a pitch is available as an open string, pitches are usually fingered on a lower string. Open strings are avoided because vibrato cannot be introduced. Nonvibrato must be indicated if that is the desired effect.

Divisi: Division of a group of like instruments into two or more parts, each with a different pitch.

Multiple stops: The simultaneous sounding of two, three, or four tones is possible on a single instrument (nondivisi). The easiest are double stops with an open string. The most difficult are triple and quadruple stops in which each note is fingered. It is impossible to bow multiple stops on other than adjacent strings or on the same string. Thirds, sixths, and tenths are highly recommended intervals. Octaves, perfect fourths, and perfect fifths are more difficult to play in tune.

Arco: Bowed; the ordinary method of tone production.

Pizzicato: Plucked with the flesh of the middle finger.

Left-hand pizzicato: Indicated by a cross (+) above the note; most effective on open strings.

Bowed tremolo: Rapid alternation of up and down bows on a single pitch. Measured tremolo consists of even division of note values and is represented by two slashes through the stem. Unmeasured tremolo, represented by three slashes, calls for uneven division of the pulse and produces a jerky effect.

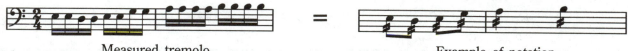
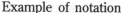

Measured tremolo   =   Example of notation

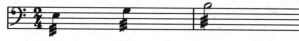

Unmeasured tremolo

FIGURE 2.1   *Bowed tremolo*

Fingered tremolo: Changing pitches; similar to a trill, but at an interval greater than a second.

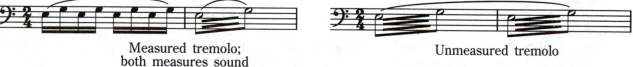

Measured tremolo;   Unmeasured tremolo
both measures sound
the same

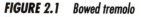

FIGURE 2.2   *Fingered tremolo*

Bariolage: Alternating between two strings; usually one is open.

Mute (sordino, Dämpfer): A small rubber device that sits on strings near the bridge or clamps onto the bridge and deadens the sound.

Sul ponticello (am Steg): Bow or pluck near the bridge.

Sul tasto (am Griffbrett): Bow or pluck over the fingerboard.

Col legno (mit Holz): Wood, rather than hair, of bow used.

Modo ordinario (ord.): Cancels effects, such as bowing in other than ordinary fashion.

Scordatura: Other than normal tuning of string; false tuning.

Glissando (portamento): Smooth slide, sounding pitches between two notes.

Natural harmonics are overtones of an open string, divided by light pressure on a node, commonly one-half, one-third, one-fourth, or one-fifth of the string's length. The pitch that sounds is notated, and a small "o" is placed over the note. If a particular string is to be used, its name is indicated (i.e., "sul G" or "sul D").

Sul D   Sul G

FIGURE 2.3   *Example of natural harmonics notated*

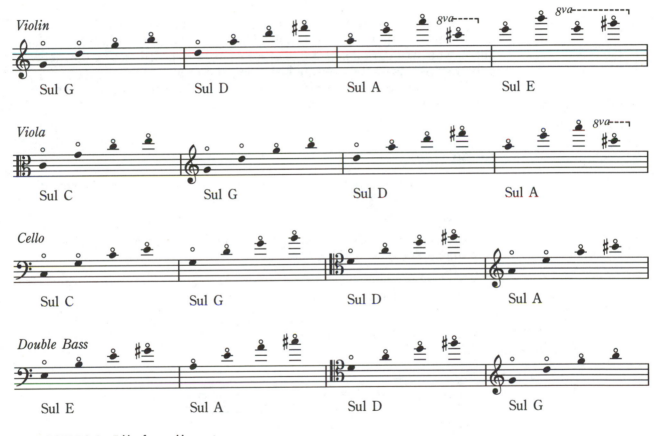

Violin

Sul G   Sul D   Sul A   Sul E

Viola

Sul C   Sul G   Sul D   Sul A

Cello

Sul C   Sul G   Sul D   Sul A

Double Bass

Sul E   Sul A   Sul D   Sul G

FIGURE 2.4   *Table of natural harmonics*

harmonics are overtones of stopped or fingered pitches; touching the perfect fourth above the stopped note produces a pitch two octaves ~~e~~ stopped note.

BOWINGS

⋇ ⊓ — symbol for downbow, placed over note

V — symbol for upbow, placed over note

Slurs are lines extending over note groupings to indicate that they are to be played under a single bow direction. These are identical to phrase markings, but short slurred groupings are interpreted as bow direction. The downbow or upbow symbol is placed over the beginning of the slur.

The tempo, dynamic levels, and character of the music dictate the types of bowing possible.

ON THE STRING

In all these bowing styles, the bow stays in constant contact with the string:

1. _Legato:_ slurred, as smooth as possible

2. _Détaché:_ each note bowed in a separate direction; may be accented or smooth; no bow markings indicated

3. _Martelé_ (hammered): a misleading term referring to "on the string" staccato; start fast, end abruptly, separate the tones

4. _Louré_ (portato): two or more notes taken on one bow, brush strokes, pushed with slight separations

FIGURE 2.6 *Example of louré bowing*

5. _Slurred staccato:_ hooked bowing; similar to louré with shorter note values

On the string

FIGURE 2.7 *Example of slurred staccato*

OFF THE STRING

Fast passages played staccato will usually be played off the string. In all of these bowing styles, the bow leaves the string:

1. *Spiccato:* midbow bounce, indicated by dots over notes, with no slurs

2. *Repeated bows:* consecutive downbow or upbow

3. *Ricochet or jeté:* throwing the bow on the string, allowing it to bounce

Off the string

FIGURE 2.8 *Staccato volante (upbow spiccato) and saltando (downbow spiccato)*

FOURTEEN BASIC PRINCIPLES OF BOW DIRECTION

  1. The note on the first beat of the measure is usually a downbow. the first note of a piece or section if it is down beat; down bow

  2. The unslurred note before the bar line (last note in a bar) is an upbow.

  3. If the note before the bar line (upbeat) is slurred across the bar line, play it downbow.

  4. An odd number of notes before a bar line (unslurred and after a rest or silence) starts an upbow.

  5. An even number of notes before a bar line (unslurred and after a rest or silence) starts a downbow.

  6. Alternate the bows (down, up) on afterbeats. If rhythmic figures between beats have an even number of notes, try a downbow on the first note; if they have an odd number of notes, try an upbow on the first note. The note with the greatest accent is played downbow.

  7. If groups of four even unslurred notes occur, starting on the beat, play the first one downbow.

  8. Link (hook) the dotted eighth and sixteenth.

  9. Do not link the dotted eighth and sixteenth in the following situations:
      a. The tempo is too fast to permit articulation.
      b. The soft passage requires extreme clarity of sound.
      c. A loud, choppy effect is desired.

 10. Link the quarter and eighth in 6/8 time.

11. Multiple stops are usually played downbow, two voices each chair.

12. If the closing chord or note has a short note before it, play the short note upbow near the frog.

13. In 4/4 time an accented half note on the second beat of the measure is taken downbow.

14. In continuous string crossing (unslurred) take the upper note upbow on violin and viola and downbow on cello and contrabass.

BOWING EXAMPLES OF THE FOURTEEN PRINCIPLES

FIGURE 2.9 *Examples of bowings according to the fourteen principles (continued on p. 26)*

9a.

9b.

9c.

10.

11.

12.

13.

14a.

14b.

ITALIAN (IT): *violino*   FRENCH (FR): *violon*   GERMAN (GER): *Violine or Geige*

E
A
D
G

PROPERTIES   The belly, or top, of the violin is made of pine or spruce, the back of maple or sycamore, the fingerboard of ebony. The E string is made of metal, and the other strings are nylon wound with a metal such as aluminum or silver. Stretching from the nut to the string holder, the strings rest upon the bridge. The violin is held under the chin with the aid of a chin rest. The bow is held in the right hand near the frog, or heel, and is strung with horsehair.

TUNING AND RANGE   Ranges on each string are determined by the player's ability and experience:

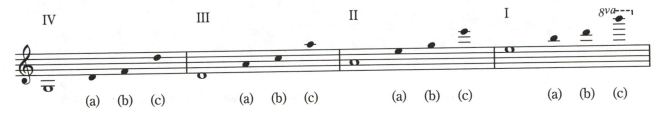

FIGURE 2.10   *Violin tuning and range, determined by the performer's ability and experience: (a) elementary, (b) intermediate, (c) professional*

TRANSPOSITION   The violin sounds as written. The treble clef is used.

TONE QUALITY   Each string has an identifiable quality compared to adjacent strings. They can be generally described as follows.

Ceiling for us octave + 3rd (10th)

G string (IV): Full, rich, dark quality; intense in the upper range

D string (III): Less full, more neutral

A string (II): Bright, singing quality

E string (I): Penetrating, piercing; used to present primary melodic material

TECHNICAL ABILITIES   Hand position is an important factor in fingering passages on the violin or any stringed instrument. The following example shows the notes available in the first three hand positions on each string.

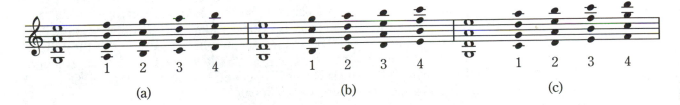

FIGURE 2.11   *The notes played by each finger in (a) first, (b) second, and (c) third positions on the violin*

Technically, there are few limitations on the violin. Situations involving string crossings and rapid shifts in position determine the difficulty, to a degree. Beginning players will have more success with music written in sharp keys. Intermediate players also experience some difficulty with intonation when dealing with numerous flats in the music.

MUSICAL EXAMPLES

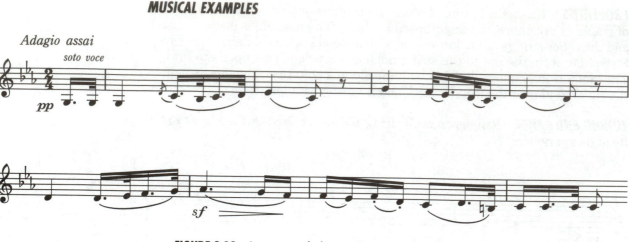

FIGURE 2.12 *Low-range violin line: Beethoven, Symphony No. 3, second movement, measures 1–8*

FIGURE 2.13 *Mid-range violin line: Beethoven, Symphony No. 9, third movement, measures 3–11*

VIOLA

IT: *viola*   FR: *alto*   GER: *Bratsche*

PROPERTIES   Much of the information regarding the violin also applies to the other stringed instruments. The viola is larger than the violin, has a darker tone quality, and has a lower range. Parts are written in alto clef in the low and middle ranges and in the treble clef in the upper range. It is technically capable of anything the violin can do. The strings are numbered from highest to lowest, I–IV. The tone quality of the low C string (IV) is warmer and has more depth than the G string (III). The D string (II) becomes somewhat brighter, and the A string (I) has good penetrating capabilities.

TUNING AND RANGE

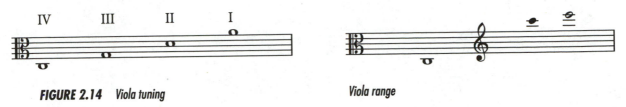

FIGURE 2.14 *Viola tuning*

Viola range

TRANSPOSITION   The viola sounds as written.

TECHNICAL ABILITIES   Although the viola is capable of executing in a lower range almost any type of passage performed on the violin, orchestral parts have not traditionally been as demanding. The viola is often relegated to static inner voices, is frequently doubled, and plays the role of the alto voice in choral music. However, many composers have taken advantage of the expressive quality of the viola as a solo voice. Berlioz was among the first to make extensive independent use of the viola in the orchestra in his *Symphonie Fantastique* in 1830. In 1834 he wrote a symphony with solo viola entitled *Harold in Italy*.

MUSICAL EXAMPLE

FIGURE 2.15   *Viola line: Berlioz, Harold in Italy, measures 38–45*

IT: *violoncello*   FR: *violoncelle*   GER: *Violoncell*

VIOLONCELLO

PROPERTIES   This instrument is commonly referred to as the cello. The open strings are tuned to the same pitches as the viola, an octave lower. The cello rests on the floor with the aid of an adjustable peg and is held between the performer's knees. It is used as both a tenor and a bass voice in the string section. Lower parts are written in the bass clef, upper parts in the tenor clef, and very high notes in the treble clef.

TUNING AND RANGE

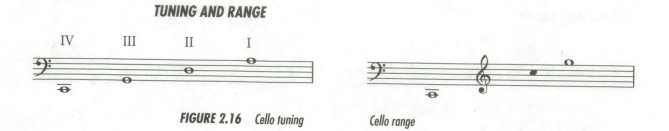

FIGURE 2.16   *Cello tuning*   *Cello range*

TRANSPOSITION   The violoncello sounds as written.

TONE QUALITY   The two lower strings have a particularly warm, mellow tone. The low C string (IV) provides a very solid bass. The G string (III) does not have as much strength or weight. The D string (II), which has a good deal of body, is most representative of the instrument. Espressivo melodies on the A string (I) have an intense, captivating quality. Flowing melodies, repeated notes, and broken chord patterns are most commonly used. Extremely versatile, the cello makes an excellent solo voice in the orchestra.

TECHNICAL ABILITIES   In the hands of a good performer the cello is a very agile instrument with few technical limitations. A difficult passage in the high range will be taken in thumb position, meaning the left thumb is used to stop the strings for fingerings at higher points on the fingerboard, something like a moveable nut. The cello is frequently coupled with other bass instruments and used to reinforce upper-register melodies an octave lower.

MUSICAL EXAMPLE

FIGURE 2.17   *Cello line: Schubert, Unfinished Symphony, measures 44–53*

DOUBLE BASS   IT: *contrabasso*   FR: *contre basse*   GER: *Kontrabass*

PROPERTIES   A member of the viol family, the double bass may have either a flat or a curved back. Viols have a more gradually sloping upper body than do instruments of the violin family. The tuning pegs are cogwheels, unlike those of other bowed strings. It is tuned in fourths rather than fifths and sounds an octave below the written pitch. The bow is shorter and wider than other string instrument bows. The German bow is widest and facilitates the underhand grip; the French style bow is held overhand like a cello bow.

TUNING AND RANGE

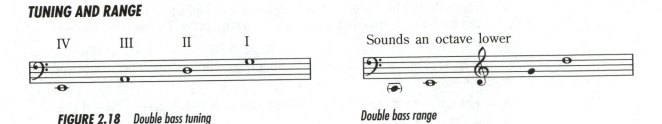

FIGURE 2.18 *Double bass tuning*   *Double bass range*

This is the true bass voice of the string section. Some European basses have five strings, the lowest tuned down to a CC. On some American basses the fourth string has an extension that enables it to be tuned down to the CC. In most cases the pitch is much clearer and more focused in its mid to upper range than in the lower register. A single double bass does not produce a very heavy sound alone, but a section of basses is quite powerful.

TECHNICAL ABILITIES   This is not an agile instrument, requiring considerable strength to play. Leaps of wide intervals, particularly in the upper range, present technical difficulties. Pizzicato is very effective. A few double stops are possible, but dividing the section is more reasonable. The section frequently doubles the cello voice an octave lower on the bass line and in general should be used relatively sparingly. Only natural harmonics are practical for the double bass.

MUSICAL EXAMPLE

Measures 1-8

Measures 141-146

FIGURE 2.19   *Double bass line: Beethoven, Symphony No. 5, third movement, measures 1–8 and 141–146*

A standard string section offers five independent groups: violins I, violins II, violas, cellos, and basses. Any of the instrumental groups may be divided, although this is not always advisable with the basses. When arranging music with a four-part harmonic texture (SATB), there are numerous doubling considerations.

SCORING FOR
THE STRING
ORCHESTRA

1. The soprano line is often doubled an octave higher by the first violins, and the bass line is doubled an octave below the cellos by the contrabasses.

2. For a full texture both inner lines might be doubled an octave above. However, it is not often advisable to double just one of the inner parts and not the other.

3. The soprano line might be doubled an octave lower in the cellos divisi.

4. Assigning both the alto and tenor lines to the violas divisi is usually weak.

5. The range and difficulty of the music and the players' ability are important factors in most scoring decisions.

The orchestrator should rely on the natural dynamics found in various registers of the instruments for best balance and mixture (i.e., a viola can be placed above the violins in a texture where it has the prominent melodic content, and the result will be very effective and striking). A theme given to the cellos in their upper register will dominate the ensemble if the violins and violas are in middle or low registers. The string section is more forgiving of wide spaces between voices than are the wind sections, due to the rich overtone content of the string timbre.

Several segments of orchestral scores are included in Appendix B to illustrate exemplary string section scoring. Refer to

1. "Eine kleine Nachtmusik," W. A. Mozart

2. Overture to *Der Freischütz,* C. M. von Weber

3. *L'Arlésienne,* Bizet (note cello range)

4. Symphony No. 5, Beethoven

5. Symphony No. 6 (*Pathétique*), Tchaikovsky

EXERCISES FOR STRING SCORING

1. Notate the open strings.

2. Rewrite for viola in alto clef.

3. Bow the cello part.

4. Score for a full string section.

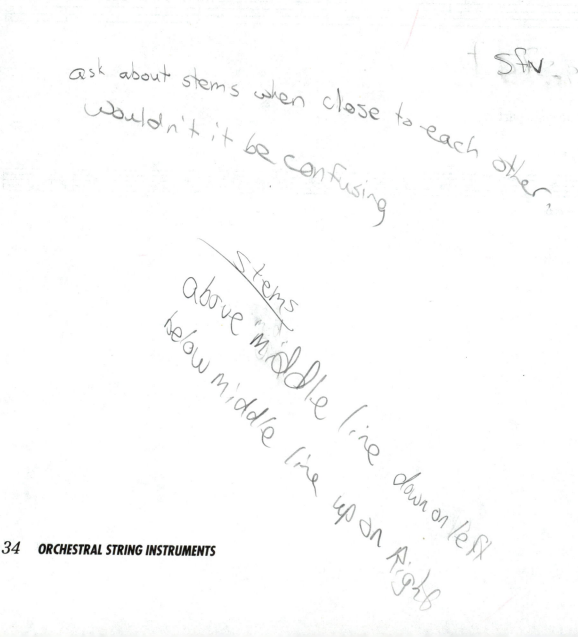

5. Define the following terms as they relate to the strings:

    a. Scordatura

    b. Double stop

    c. Pizzicato

    d. Sul tasto

    e. Artificial harmonics

    f. Bratsche

    g. Senza sordino

    h. Col legno

    i. Divisi

    j. Arco

6. Indicate "on the string" or "off the string" for the following bowings:

    a. Spiccato _____   e. Legato _____

    b. Louré _____   f. Saltando _____

    c. Jeté _____   g. Martelé _____

    d. Détaché _____

7. Indicate whether the following statements are true (T) or false (F):

    a. _____ Tempo markings and dynamics are both written below the staff in the orchestral score and parts.

    b. _____ The double bass sounds two octaves below the written note.

    c. _____ String players usually play with vibrato, unless otherwise specified.

    d. _____ In general, notes on the double bass are clearest and have the best definition in its lowest register.

    e. _____ In second position on the violin, the first finger plays B on the G string.

    f. _____ Fingered tremolo is the equivalent of a trill at an interval larger than a second.

    g. _____ To begin a downbow the frog is farthest from the string.

Chapter Three

Woodwind Instruments

Since Beethoven's time, a typical orchestral woodwind section has consisted of flutes, oboes, clarinets, and bassoons in pairs. One of the players may be required to double on another instrument in the same family, such as the piccolo, English horn, bass clarinet, or contrabassoon. A larger woodwind section maintains the pairs, with auxiliary performers on the added instruments.

As a rule each pair of instruments shares a staff in the score. If two notes sound simultaneously, the first player takes the upper note, and the second takes the lower. In the case of a single note line played by both instruments, the indication "a2" must be placed over the music, or stems must be placed in both directions from the notes. When a single note line is played by one instrument, the indication "1." or "2." must be placed over the music, or rests must be placed above or below the line. The indication "a2" is not needed in passages with two separate parts. Orchestral woodwinds do not use divisi or unisono, terms reserved for string and band players. If the part is a solo, it should be indicated as such and will usually be taken by the first chair. Label an entering voice with 1. or 2. and a dynamic marking if the other chair is already playing.

Two oboes play unison in (a) and the first measure of (b). In the second measure of (b) they split.

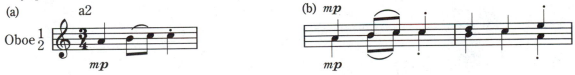

Only the first oboe plays in (c) and the first measure of (d). The second oboe enters in the second measure of (d).

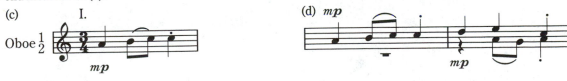

FIGURE 3.1   *Two parts sharing a staff*

WOODWIND ARTICULATION

Each note will be tongued, or enunciated, separately if it is not slurred with another note. A staccato tongue resembles the syllable "tu"; a legato tongue resembles "du." A slur marking is not placed over repeated notes on the same pitch, unless an articulation mark is placed over each. The interpretation of articulation markings depends on style and context. In most modern usage the articulation on the left below requests more separation than the one on the right.

FIGURE 3.2 *Articulations*

It is generally best to indicate slurring rather than phrasing and to use breath marks where needed for the woodwinds. Double-tonguing, useful in passages too rapid to be single-tongued, is used primarily on the flute. Double-tonguing consists of alternating syllables: "tu-ku-tu-ku." Triple-tonguing is useful for fast triplet patterns; it sounds like the syllables "tu-tu-ku" or "tu-ku-tu." Flutter tonguing is a special effect produced by rolling an "r-r-r" in the throat while producing a tone. A sforzando attack (sfz) is possible within the context of any dynamic level.

FLUTE

IT: *flauto*   FR: *flûte*   GER: *Flöte*

PROPERTIES   The flute is a cylindrical metal pipe $26\frac{1}{2}$ inches long with a $\frac{3}{4}$-inch inner diameter. The player blows across the side hole (or embouchure) to cause the air in the pipe to vibrate. Pitches in the lowest octave are fundamentals on the flute.

RANGE AND NATURAL DYNAMICS

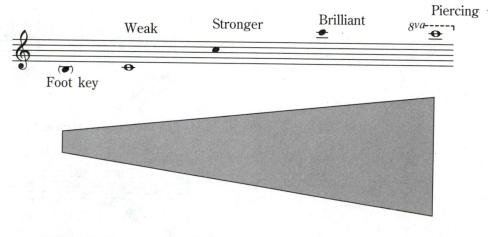

FIGURE 3.3 *Flute range*

The compass is from c¹ upwards approximately three octaves, getting progressively brighter and more powerful. Some flutes have a foot key that adds 2 inches in length, enabling them to sound the b below c¹.

TONE QUALITY   The flute's pure tone quality, lacking in overtones, makes it combine well with other instruments. Lower notes are breathy and upper notes penetrating; the range is otherwise quite even. It is easily covered unless exposed; notes in the lower octave are lost when combined with several instruments pitched lower. Having a unique timbre, the flute is effectively used in its very low range when it does not have to compete with other instruments to be heard.

TECHNICAL ABILITIES   This the most agile wind instrument, capable of wide leaps, filigree, arpeggios, trills, and rapid repeated notes. The flute requires a great deal of breath support and lip tension, so frequent rests are important for best results. Double-, triple-, and flutter tonguing (like a rolled "r") are possible. Unplayable trills and tremolos are as follows:

FIGURE 3.4   *Unplayable trills*

Other members of the flute family include:

Piccolo (It: ottavino): Half the size of the flute, the piccolo sounds an octave higher. The lowest note available is d¹, and in the upper register it can become a shrill whistle.

Alto flute: Approximately one-third larger than the flute, the alto flute sounds a perfect fourth lower than written. It is sometimes called the G flute because the g below c¹ is the pitch that sounds when a written c¹ is played.

Bass flute: Rarely used except in flute choirs, it sounds an octave below written pitch.

Piccolo   Alto   and Bass Flutes

FIGURE 3.5   *Piccolo, alto, and bass flute ranges*

FIGURE 3.6 Flute line: Beethoven, *Leonore* Overture No. 3, measures 328–337

Refer also to Appendix B, the first movement of Dvořák's *New World* Symphony.

OBOE

IT: *oboe*   FR: *hautbois*   GER: *Oboe, Hoboe*

PROPERTIES   The oboe is a wooden double-reed instrument with a conical bore. Two curved blades of cane are bound around a staple, which is inserted in the upper end of the oboe to form the mouthpiece. The reeds vibrating together at their elliptical opening produce the tone. Slight differences in moisture or temperature or imperfections in the reed can have an enormous effect on the tone. The oboe is overblown at the octave.

RANGE AND NATURAL DYNAMICS

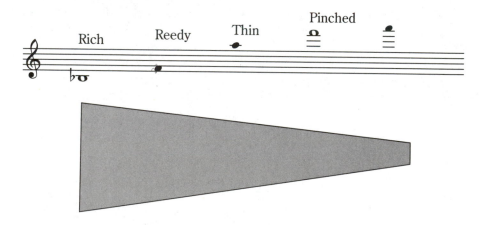

FIGURE 3.7 Oboe range

The compass is roughly two and a half octaves upward from b♭ below c¹. It is very difficult to play the lowest notes quietly and delicately.

TONE QUALITY   The middle register is reedy and characteristic. The oboe generally penetrates through other instrumental textures, so it makes an excellent solo voice. A moderate amount of vibrato is a standard element in the oboe sound. Because of its striking tone color, the oboe should be used sparingly.

TECHNICAL ABILITIES   The oboe is an extremely agile instrument, capable of performing complex passages. It requires considerable breath support in the lungs because the small quantity of air that moves through the instrument must be carefully controlled. Beginning a phrase on a very low note is quite difficult. Rests should occur frequently in oboe parts to allow the player to take in fresh oxygen. Fast single-tonguing is possible, but double-tonguing is very difficult. All trills are possible, as are tremolos between notes up to about a perfect fourth apart, on professional quality instruments. There are some limitations in this area on student models.

MUSICAL EXAMPLE

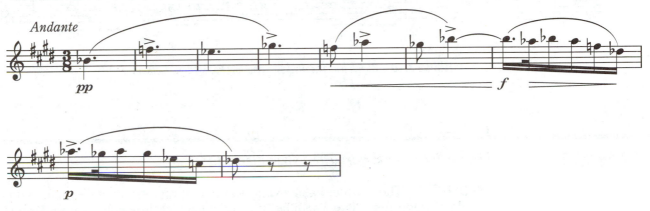

FIGURE 3.8   *Oboe line: Schubert, Unfinished Symphony, Andante, measures 84–92*

Refer also to the Overture to *Der Freischütz* by C. M. von Weber in Appendix B.

It: *corno inglese*   Fr: *cor anglais*   Ger: *englisches Horn*   **ENGLISH HORN**

RANGE AND NATURAL DYNAMICS

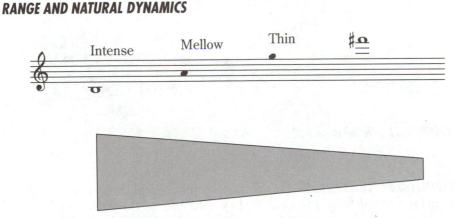

FIGURE 3.9   *English horn range*

TRANSPOSITION   The English horn is pitched in F and must be transposed up a perfect fifth in the treble clef. The compass is two and a half octaves upwards from the b below c¹. Oboe and English horn share a similar dynamic curve, and common principles govern their use. The lowest tones on the English horn are produced much more easily and gracefully than on the oboe. It has a more delicate, rounded sound throughout its range and blends more readily with other instruments, but it is somewhat less agile. The term "English" may be a mistranslation of the French word "angle" because the instrument was initially curved and is not of English origin.

Less common members of the oboe family are the oboe d'amore, the baritone oboe, and the heckelphone.

MUSICAL EXAMPLE

FIGURE 3.10   *English horn line: Dvořák, Symphony No. 9, Largo, measures 7–10*

CLARINET

IT: *clarinetto*   FR: *clarinette*   GER: *Klarinette*

PROPERTIES   The clarinet has a cylindrical bore, employs a single reed, and is made of wood (usually grenadilla). It is overblown at the twelfth rather than at the octave. Odd numbered harmonics are strongly emphasized. The clarinet has the acoustical properties of a stopped pipe, with the fundamental an octave lower than an open pipe or a conical pipe of the same length.

RANGE AND NATURAL DYNAMICS

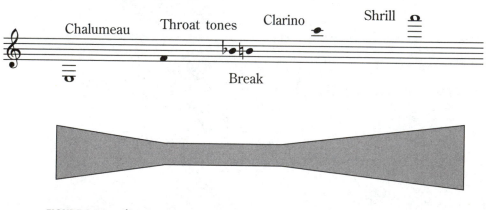

FIGURE 3.11   *Clarinet range*

TRANSPOSITION   The B♭ clarinet is the most common, and the part is transposed UP a major second from the concert key. Because of this transposition, it is more easily handled in concert keys with flats. The A clarinet is also used frequently by orchestral performers, and the transposition is UP a minor third.

A has fewer accidentals to deal with when used in concert keys with sharps. The compass of the clarinet is from e upwards approximately three and a half octaves.

TONE QUALITY   The chalumeau register, which consists of the lowest octave of the range, is surprisingly strong and warm. The throat tones in the middle register are weaker, but the clarino register becomes very bright and incisive. The highest register is brilliant and penetrating. The tone of the upper register is less characteristic and quite flutelike. Extremely wide dynamic variations are possible on pitches throughout the majority of the clarinet's range. The sound below the break is easily covered by other instruments. When chords for woodwinds are being orchestrated in a high tessitura, the clarinet is best placed above the oboes; in lower harmonies it may be best to score it below the oboes.

TECHNICAL ABILITIES   The clarinet is extremely agile, capable of fast runs, arpeggios, trills, wide leaps, and expressive legato. It may be wise to avoid assigning it melodic passages that hover around the break. Double-tonguing is possible but used only in very rapid tempi. A sharp staccato is available, as well as a semidetached articulation similar to the louré bowings on stringed instruments. All trills are accomplished easily by means of many alternate fingerings. Vibrato is not normally used in orchestral playing.

MUSICAL EXAMPLE

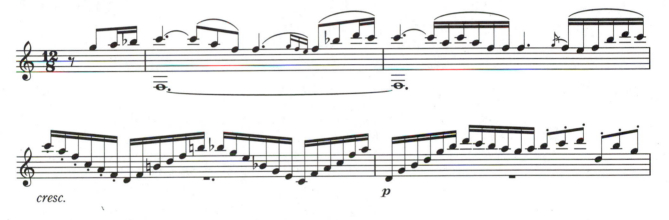

FIGURE 3.12   *Clarinet line: Beethoven, Symphony No. 6, second movement, measures 69–72. (Note the articulative nature of the solo part and the low register tone held by the second clarinet.)*

Refer to Appendix B, Tchaikovsky's Symphony No. 6, and the second movement of the Dvořák *New World* Symphony, for other clarinet excerpts.

B♭ BASS CLARINET

IT: *clarinetto basso*   FR: *clarinette basse*   GER: *Bassklarinette*

The range and facilities of the B♭ bass clarinet are similar to other clarinets, but it has a curve near the mouthpiece and an upturned bell and is twice the length of the B♭ clarinet. The instrumental part is written in the treble clef and must be transposed UP a major ninth from concert pitch. In older German scores the part was often written in the bass clef and transposed UP a major second from sounding pitch. The lowest written note is e♭, but on a few instruments the c an octave below c¹ is available. Although the upper register is weak and seldom used, the middle and lower registers are common in solo and doubling applications. Considerable control of volume levels and dynamic nuances are possible on the bass clarinet.

E♭ CLARINETS

All E♭ clarinet parts are written in the treble clef. The following are members of this family.

SOPRANO CLARINET IN E♭ This instrument is used in concert bands and can be found in some orchestral scores (the *Symphonie Fantastique* by Berlioz and *Till Eulenspiegel* by Richard Strauss). A smaller version of the B♭ clarinet, it transposes DOWN a minor third. It has a thin, squeaky tone, is difficult to control in its extreme upper and lower registers, and has a penetrating quality in the high register.

ALTO CLARINET IN E♭ A standard member of the concert band, this is rarely used in the orchestra. Transposition is UP a major sixth from sounding to written pitch. Soft, low parts for the instrument will often be covered by the ensemble.

CONTRABASS CLARINET IN E♭ This larger version of the bass clarinet is called for in some concert band scores. Parts are transposed UP an octave plus a major sixth.

BASSOON

IT: *fagotto*   FR: *basson*   GER: *Fagott*

PROPERTIES The bassoon is a double-reed, conical bore instrument most often made of maple wood, although plastic and hard rubber are also used. The pipe is bent double, and the reed is attached to a tube called the bocal, which curves away from the instrument. The instrument provides a bass or tenor voice for the woodwind choir.

RANGE AND NATURAL DYNAMICS

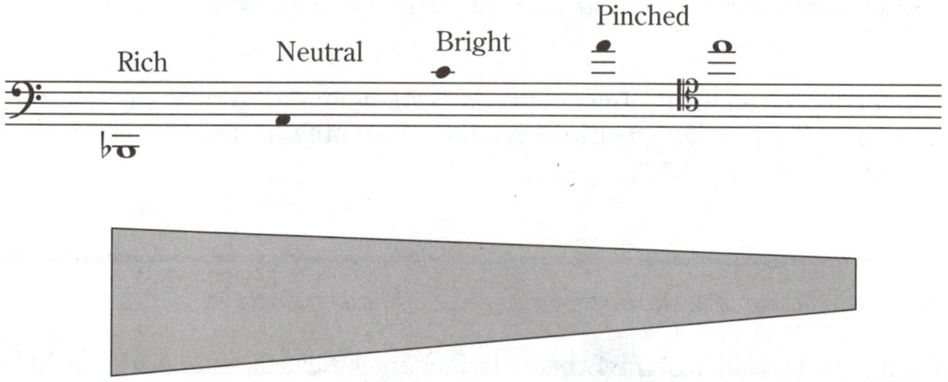

FIGURE 3.13 *Bassoon range*

TRANSPOSITION The bassoon sounds as written. The compass is from BB♭ upwards approximately three and a half octaves. As in all double reeds, the dynamics are strong in the low extremes of the range and progressively weaker in the upper registers. The bass clef is used for passages in the low and middle parts of the range; the tenor clef is used for passages in the highest part.

TONE QUALITY The bassoon's timbre is much less nasal than that of the oboe, but it has the capacity to produce similar articulations. The lowest register is dark and rich in overtones, and very soft notes with delicate attacks are difficult to produce in this range. The middle range is transparent, blending well with other instruments, and very expressive. The upper register, which makes a unique solo voice, does not penetrate through a heavy texture.   In the hands of an accomplished player, the entire range is quite even and suitable for unobtrusive accompanimental parts or solos with a light background.

TECHNICAL ABILITIES Except in extreme low and high ranges, the bassoon is agile. Wide leaps and rapid tonguing are idiomatic. In writing for the bassoon, orchestrators should provide ample rests in very loud or very low passages. Notes are usually single-tongued, but all other tonguings are possible. Some trills (major or minor second) are problematic in extreme high and low registers, as are rapid repeated notes in the lowest part of the range.

MUSICAL EXAMPLE

pp

FIGURE 3.14 *Bassoon line: Beethoven, Symphony No. 5, second movement, measures 205-213*

CONTRABASSOON

The contrabassoon sounds an octave lower than the bassoon and is slightly less agile. Its practical range is approximately two and a half octaves upwards from the low BB♭, and the highest part of the range is seldom used. The powerful, incisive sound is useful in dense textures to strengthen the bass line. Obsolete members of the bassoon family include the tenoroon, the quartfagott, and the quintfagott.

SAXOPHONE

IT: *sassofono*   FR: *saxophone*   GER: *Saxophon*

PROPERTIES Saxophones are made of brass and employ a single reed. They have stopped conical pipes, which overblow at the octave like open cylindrical pipes. The soprano saxophone may be a straight or curved pipe; alto, tenor, and baritone saxophones all curve to the mouthpiece and have upturned bells.

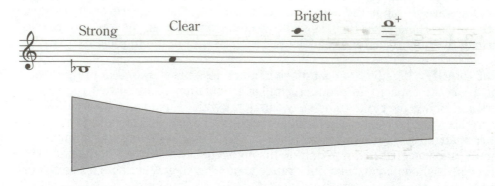

FIGURE 3.15 *Saxophone range*

TRANSPOSITION   From sounding to written pitch, saxophone transpositions are as follows:

B♭ soprano—UP a major second

E♭ alto—UP a major sixth

B♭ tenor—UP a major ninth

E♭ baritone—UP an octave and major sixth

The compass of all the saxophones is from b♭ upwards two and a half octaves. Professional players can use another octave above this, the "altissimo" register, where irregular fingerings are employed and good lip control is required.

TONE QUALITY   Tones in the lowest fifth of the saxophone's range are difficult to produce softly, and the response is hard to control. This effect is not as pronounced on the tenor and baritone saxophones. The alto saxophone, the most frequently used, has a fluid, hornlike quality with the attack of a reed. The tenor has a deeper and more penetrating "reedy" tone. The baritone is somewhat mellower than the tenor and provides a good bass voice for the family. With a nasal edge, the soprano is somewhat similar in tone and design to the oboe. Saxophones blend well with one another and balance with brass instruments.

Many French composers, such as Bizet, Ravel, and Milhaud, have included the E♭ alto saxophone in their orchestral works, as have Berg, Prokofiev, Copland, Britten, and Vaughan Williams. Although much of the music written for the instrument is from French chamber and wind literature, there are over two thousand works that include saxophone in the orchestral repertoire. Saxophones are not a standard component in the orchestra, but a quartet consisting of two altos, a tenor, and a baritone is used consistently in concert bands and wind ensembles.

TECHNICAL ABILITIES   The saxophones are extremely agile. All types of figures are practical, but rapid repeated notes are probably the most difficult. Trills in the altissimo register are very awkward, as are those between low C^1 and B♭.

Performers who double on various saxophones benefit from the different transposition for each. The music is transposed for each instrument so that fingerings for written pitches on any type of saxophone are the same. Because the written ranges are also the same, the alto player can perform on the tenor or baritone with a minor change of embouchure.

MUSICAL EXAMPLE

FIGURE 3.16   E♭ alto saxophone line: Bizet, L'Arlésienne Suite No. 1, Prelude, measures 91–98

EXERCISES FOR WOODWIND SCORING

1. Score for the woodwind section.

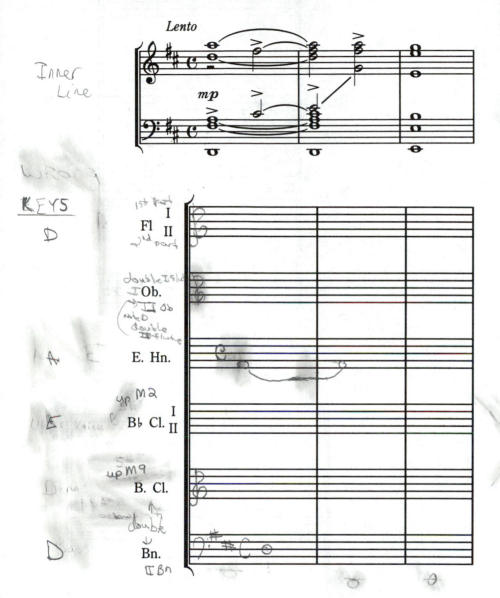

2. Score for the instruments requested, providing key signature and clef for each.

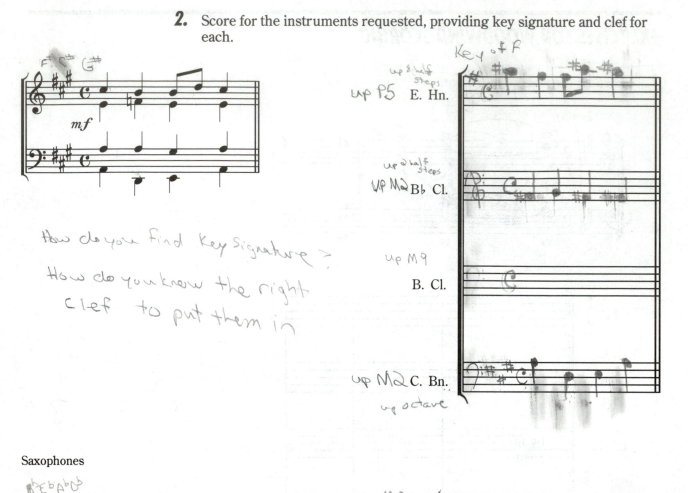

How do you find key signature?

How do you know the right clef to put them in

Saxophones

3. Circle the answer that best describes the two statements:

A   Only the first statement is true.
B   Only the second statement is true.
Both   Both statements are true.
Neither   Neither statement is true.

a.   The bass clarinet part is written in the treble clef.
     The baritone saxophone part is written in the treble clef.
        A   B   Both   Neither

b.   In its highest range the bassoon part is written in the tenor clef.
     The English horn sounds a perfect fifth lower than written.
        A   B   Both   Neither

c.   The piccolo sounds an octave higher than written.
     The bassoon sounds an octave lower than written.
        A   B   Both   Neither

d.   The woodwinds will tongue each note, unless a slur is indicated.
     The notation "a2" is used over a staff with two similar instruments playing different notes.
        A   B   Both   Neither

e.   If a single line is written for clarinets sharing a staff, either 1. or 2. must be used.
     An alternative to this indication is placing rests above or below.
        A   B   Both   Neither

f.   Triple-tonguing might sound like the syllables "tu-tu-ku."
     Flutter tonguing can be produced only by the flutes; no other woodwind has the capacity.
        A   B   Both   Neither

g.   The flute and clarinet both have a conical bore.
     The lowest written note for the B♭ clarinet is the lowest sounding note for an English horn.
        A   B   Both   Neither

4. List the orchestral woodwinds in the order they would appear in a score. Place an "X" beside the instruments that would not typically occur in pairs.

_____   1. _____

_____   2. _____

_____   3. _____

_____   4. _____

_____   5. _____

_____   6. _____

_____   7. _____

_____   8. _____

Chapter Four

Brass Instruments

Sound is produced on all brass instruments by the performer's lips, which vibrate together to make a buzz. The instrument becomes a resonating chamber when the column of air in the instrument is excited by this buzz. The tubing is made of brass, and the flared bell radiates the sound. Lip tension determines the pitch, greater lip tension producing higher harmonics based on the fundamental determined by the instrument's length.

Before valves were commonly used with brass instruments, natural horns and trumpets were limited to pitches in the harmonic series, which explains how music was written for early brass. The length of the column of air could be altered by the use of "crooks," or additional short pieces of tubing inserted into the instrument. Some composers called for combinations of brass instruments pitched in different keys at once. Tuning slides were common on many brass instruments; these allowed the player to tune the fundamental down by a half step on short notice. Parts were typically written in the key of C, and the length of the crook determined the sounding pitch. Review Chapter One for the distance and direction of transposition for the various natural horns and trumpets.

By the middle of the eighteenth century, horn players had adopted the practice of inserting their hand into the bell of the horn, lowering the pitch by a semitone or a whole tone to produce notes other than those available in a given overtone series. Varying the length of the tube by means of valves was introduced circa 1815, and modern valved brass became quite different from their predecessors. The older trumpets, for example, were twice as long as their newer counterparts and sounded an octave lower.

The trumpet has penetrating power in its upper register, but in the middle to low registers it can be played softly and blends well. Having a wide dynamic range throughout its compass, the trombone can be an assertive voice or blend well with other instruments in any register. The horns, due to their conical bore, length of tubing, and shape of mouthpiece, are not as strong. A popular adage is that it requires a pair of horns at a moderate to loud volume level to balance with one trumpet and one trombone if all instruments are in their middle registers. Orchestrators should allow brass instruments to lead up to high pitches, rather than asking them to hit high notes without preparation. In this respect treating brass performers as one would treat vocalists is wise. Chords scored for trumpets and horns generally sound better in close spacing than in open position, as is also true of trombones together in their upper register. A wide interval between second and third (bass) trombone also produces a good sound from the section.

THE BRASS SECTION

53

SPECIAL EFFECTS FOR BRASS INSTRUMENTS

Vibrato: Alternate small variations in pitch above and below the actual center of a tone. This is not a normal aspect of traditional orchestral brass technique. Three types of vibrato are possible: diaphragm, jaw, and mechanical. The jaw vibrato is most commonly used.

Lip trill: Vacillate between two pitches by tightening and loosening the embouchure; no change in fingering or slide position is made. Lip trills are most effective in the upper register, where consecutive overtones are closer together.

Glissando: Slide smoothly between two pitches, sounding some or all of the pitches that lie between. It may move upwards or downwards.

Brassy tone (It: metallizzare i suoni, Fr: cuivre, Ger: schmettern): Produce a strident, forced sound with metallic quality. This is used only at loud dynamic levels.

Bells up (It: campana in aria, Fr: pavillon en l'air, Ger: Schalltrichter auf): Raise the bell for better projection as well as the visual effect.

Multiphonics: Play one pitch and hum another.

TYPES OF MUTES USED BY BRASS INSTRUMENTS

Straight: Most common, made of metal or cardboard; produces a bright, pungent sound. This type is used when the term "muted" is indicated for orchestral brass.

Cup: Produces a colorless, nasal sound without any edge.

Mica: Similar to the cup mute, but mellower with a little more natural sustain.

Harmon: Metal mute with an adjustable stem; sound has a sharp edge.

Bucket: Also called Velvetone; used for mellow, soft sound with no edge.

Whispa: The softest mute; absorbs the sound.

Solotone: Rarely found; the tone is nasal with some bite.

Mutes make instruments more difficult to play. Conservative passages that avoid extremes of range work best when mutes are applied. *Allow sufficient time to insert and remove the mute.* Two measures at a moderate tempo is plenty, assuming the player is prepared. Brass instruments may also be muted by playing into the stand or by covering the bell with the hand, a hat, or a plunger.

HORN

It: *corno*   Fr: *cor*   Ger: *Horn*

PROPERTIES   The horn is a conical coiled tube with a cup-shaped mouthpiece and widely flared bell. The double horn, with three valves, is most common. It is pitched in F, and the thumb operates a valve that changes the fundamental to B♭ a perfect fourth higher. This option facilitates performance in the upper range, where overtones of the shorter fundamental are more easily distinguished.

RANGE AND NATURAL DYNAMICS

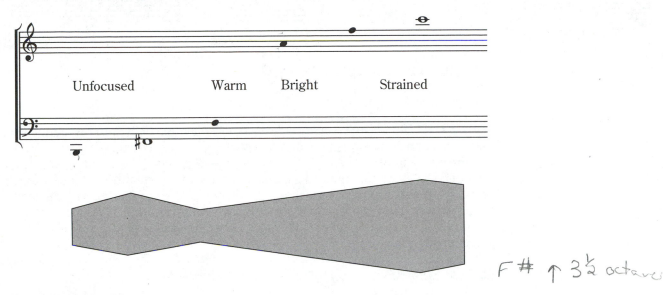

F# ↑ 3½ octaves

FIGURE 4.1 *Horn range*

TRANSPOSITION Transpose UP a perfect fifth, writing in treble clef as much as possible. Some older notation transposed the part a perfect fourth lower when using bass clef. This method is not used currently, but a note regarding the transposition method used in the score may be added to avoid confusion. The compass is from F♯ upwards approximately three and a half octaves. The horn is seldom used in its extreme upper or lower ranges.

TONE QUALITY The notes are not solid in the lower octave and are easily covered by other instruments. The horn's presence is felt more than heard in this register. The middle two octaves are characteristically dark and heroic. The higher notes get progressively brighter and sound somewhat forced. The unobtrusive quality of the horn makes it a popular accompanimental voice in the alto range, but it can become monotonous if overused in this fashion. The upper register is used for solo work.

TECHNICAL ABILITIES One of the more difficult instruments to master, the horn is not particularly agile. Lip and valve trills are possible but difficult. Wide leaps should be used cautiously, as should fast running passages. Allow sufficient rests for breathing and for relaxing the lip muscles. Intonation and attack depend on the performer's ability to "hear" the desired pitch, and lines should be smoothly designed. Traditionally, horn players have been more often assigned the fifth of a chord rather than the third in stationary harmonies. A number of challenging solos can be found in the literature for the instrument, such as those written by Richard Strauss in *Till Eulenspiegel*.

There is a "division of labor" peculiar to the horn section. The first and third horns play the higher parts while the second and fourth horns play the lower parts. An interlocking voicing pattern is used when scoring chords for the horns. Doubling of pairs is very common, as is the use of a powerful unison for all horns. Another practice maintained in horn sections is the presence of an assistant first player, who may be called upon at any time to share the demanding duties of the first part.

FIGURE 4.2   *Ranges and interlocking voicing*

SPECIAL EFFECTS   Players normally insert their hand partially into the bell, cupping it to control tone quality and pitch. Muting can be accomplished by inserting the hand into the bell, producing "stopped" tones. The notation for this effect is a "+" over the notes. To indicate a return to normal open tones, some orchestrators place an "o" over the notes. Stopped tones are nasal, with an edge to the sound. They are particularly effective when used on forte-piano single notes and in exposed passages. The indication "lontano" asks the performer for a distant-sounding tone.

MUSICAL EXAMPLES

FIGURE 4.3   *Horn line: Tchaikovsky, Symphony No. 5, second movement, measures 8–12*

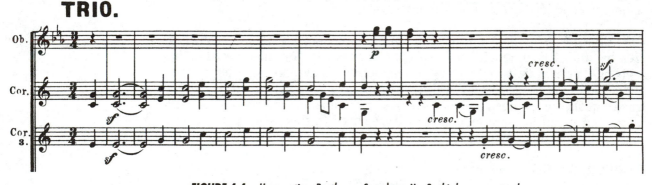

FIGURE 4.4   *Horn section: Beethoven, Symphony No. 3, third movement, scherzo*

TRUMPET

IT: *tromba*   FR: *trompette*   GER: *Trompete*

PROPERTIES   The trumpet is thought of as having a primarily cylindrical bore, although modern instruments are conical toward both ends. They are made of brass and have three piston valves and a small tuning slide that adjusts the pitch of the entire instrument. The first and third valves each have their own tuning slides. A cup-shaped mouthpiece is used. The first valve lowers the pitch by a whole step, the second valve by a half step, and the third by a minor third.

RANGE AND NATURAL DYNAMICS

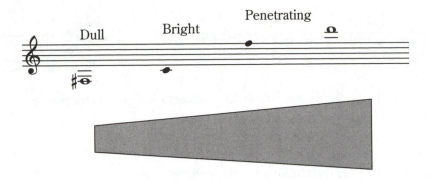

FIGURE 4.5   *Trumpet range*

TRANSPOSITION

B♭ trumpet (common)—UP a major second.

C trumpet (gaining popularity)—sounds as written

D trumpet (rare)—DOWN a major second.

E♭ trumpet (rare)—DOWN a minor third

The compass of the trumpet is from f♯ upwards approximately two and one half octaves. Some players, such as those in jazz bands, can play effectively for another octave above this range.

TONE QUALITY   The extreme low register is difficult to control, dull and metallic, and may tend to "blat" in the hands of an inexperienced player. Notes in the middle and lower ranges (around c¹), which can be played softly, blend well with most instruments. The trumpet is most often used in its middle range, where it is forceful and brilliant. As pitches get higher, the tone is increasingly penetrating, and great skill is required to play pianissimo in the highest range. Orchestrators should lead up to high notes and not stay in the upper range for too long. Because a solo trumpet can dominate an orchestral tutti, the powerful tone should be used with discretion.

TECHNICAL ABILITIES   The trumpet is the most agile of the brass instruments. Rapid passages, wide leaps in either direction, arpeggios, and double- or triple-tongued repeated notes are part of the solo technique. All trills are possible, as are tremolos, but their speed is limited by cross-fingerings (one finger is depressed and another released simultaneously). Lip trills are used for notes above the staff. Fanfares are most characteristic, and the incisive tone lends itself to crisp, assertive passages.

FIGURE 4.6 *Trumpet line for trumpets in E: Dvořák, Symphony No. 9, allegro con fuoco, measures 18–25, in octaves*

Other members of the trumpet family include:

Cornet: The cornet is similar to the trumpet, mellower in sound, and usually pitched in B♭ with the same range and capabilities. Traditionally of conical bore, cornets are growing more similar in shape to the trumpet, with a larger bore and a more flared bell. They are a mainstay in military and concert bands.

Flugelhorn: The flugelhorn has a conical bore and darker sound but is similar to the trumpet in range and capabilities. The lower register is fuller and more similar in timbre to the horn than the trumpet.

Piccolo and bass trumpets: These are the smallest and largest members of the family, respectively. Pitched in a variety of keys, they are used for special effects and for extremes of range. Many Baroque trumpet parts require the higher range of the piccolo trumpet.

F alto trumpet: This was the standard nineteenth-century orchestral instrument, often used with adjustable tubing. It was called for frequently by Tchaikovsky, Mahler, and Richard Strauss.

TROMBONE

IT: *trombone* FR: *trombone* GER: *Posaune*

PROPERTIES The trombone is a cylindrical brass tube folded back on itself twice into which a cup mouthpiece is inserted. A slide mechanism is used to lengthen the tubing. With the slide in first position, the fundamental is pitched in B♭. An F attachment provides a trigger to lower the fundamental a perfect fourth, eliminating awkward slide position changes.

RANGE AND NATURAL DYNAMICS

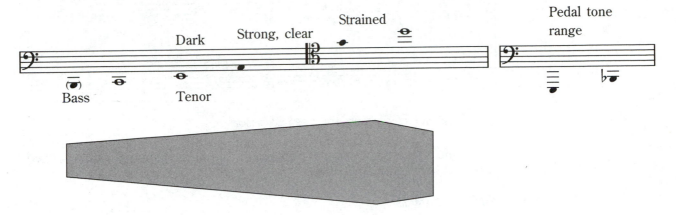

FIGURE 4.7   *Trombone range*

TRANSPOSITION   The trombone sounds as written. Bass clef is used primarily, but tenor clef may be employed for extended high passages. The compass of the tenor trombone extends from E below the staff upwards approximately two and a half octaves. Many modern tenor trombones are equipped with an F attachment, in which case their range begins on C and extends upwards almost three octaves. The bass trombone has a larger bore and a wider bell, its upper register is not used as often as that of the tenor trombone, and it is more frequently called upon to sound pedal tones, the actual fundamental pitch found in each slide position. The fuzzy growl of the pedal tone is something of a special effect, first used by Berlioz in his *Requiem*. In addition to an F attachment, many bass trombones have an E attachment, which extends the range down to BB. Attachments altering the fundamental to E♭, G, and G♭ are also available for trombones.

TONE QUALITY   The tone is full, rich, and dignified through the range. The instrument is capable of wide dynamic variations at any pitch level, balances exceedingly well with all other instruments, and has the power to be heard in any context. Trombones work well in open or closed voicings and perform sustained chords in accompaniment very well. The modern trombone is one of the most versatile instruments in the orchestra.

TECHNICAL ABILITIES   Dexterity is very good in the upper range, where alternative positions for many notes are available. In lower ranges agility is limited by rapid slide movements, a problem largely alleviated by using the F attachment. Legato notes are tongued lightly, and rapid short figures and repeated notes work well. Double-, triple-, and flutter tonguings are possible. Frequent rests are helpful because the instrument requires a lot of air. Wide leaps are somewhat out of character, and tremolos are simply not possible. Lip trills or valve trills with the use of the trigger are the only type of trills available. A short glissando, within the length of slide in either direction, is a common effect. Instances of a solo trombone given the melody are relatively rare in the symphonic literature. The alto trombone, which is no longer in use, was a standard member of the trombone choir in the eighteenth and nineteenth centuries. The trombone was not used in symphonic literature until Beethoven's Fifth Symphony.

FIGURE 4.8   Chart showing notes in each slide position

Avoid successive rapid slide movement between distant positions—low B♭ to B, first to seventh positions.

MUSICAL EXAMPLE

FIGURE 4.9   Trombone line: Beethoven, Symphony No. 9, fourth movement, measures 1–9

Refer to Appendix B, the fourth movement of Brahms's First Symphony, for a classic example of trombone writing.

TUBA

IT: *tuba*   FR: *tuba*   GER: *Basstuba*

tuba   tuba   Basstuba

PROPERTIES   The tuba has a large, conical bore and either three or four valves of rotary or piston design. The fourth valve is used to adjust intonation with other valve combinations. Tubas are also available with five or six valves. The most common shape is with upright bell, but some student models are bell front, and marching bands may use the helicon design. All have deep cup mouthpieces.

Concert Pitch B♭♭

RANGE AND NATURAL DYNAMICS

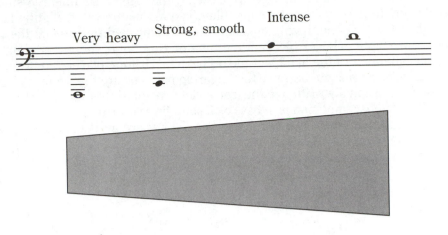

FIGURE 4.10 *Tuba range*

TRANSPOSITION Tubas are nontransposing; they sound as written. Bass clef and ledger lines are always used (not 8va). The compass is from DD upwards approximately three octaves. The most common tubas are the double C and double B♭ (also called contrabass tuba). The tuba in F is smaller and a bit brighter.

[handwritten: DD ↑ 3 octaves]

TONE QUALITY The tuba's sound is rich and expressive throughout its range. Lower pitches lack focus, and higher pitches sound strained. A velvety piano and powerful forte are available at most pitch levels.

TECHNICAL ABILITIES The tuba is very agile, notwithstanding its size, and can articulate rapidly. Wide leaps and rapid passage work are possible, but slow, sustained writing is more characteristic. Because a great deal of breath is required, ample rests should be employed. Blending well with all the instruments, it is often combined in unison with double bass or bassoon.

MUSICAL EXAMPLE

FIGURE 4.11 *Tuba line: Richard Strauss, Also Sprach Zarathustra, nine measures after rehearsal number 50, two tubas in octaves with trombones*

A memorable excerpt featuring the tuba can be found in Wagner's *Die Meistersinger* nine measures after letter J.

EUPHONIUM AND BARITONE

The euphonium and baritone are basically the same instrument. A smaller member of the tuba family, the euphonium is often made with a slightly larger bore than the baritone. It employs four valves, compared to three on the baritone. More agile and flexible than the tuba or trombone, the euphonium is a standard member of the band, not the orchestra. Baritone players are frequently former cornet players because the fingering patterns are the same, and band parts are occasionally written in the treble clef a major ninth higher for the baritone. The standard notation is in bass clef, sounding as written, and the range is the same as that of the tenor trombone. Pedal tones are available on each valve position in the lowest register.

3. List the instruments of the brass section as they would appear in an orchestral score, the usual numbers of each, and the distance and direction of transposition for each.

_____ # _____ transpose _____

_____ # _____ transpose _____

_____ # _____ transpose _____

_____ # _____ transpose _____

4. Answer the following questions as concisely and completely as possible.

   a. Describe the "division of labor" within the horn section and how dynamics and range would affect doublings to balance with other brass instruments.

   b. Describe the difference in timbre between brass instruments with a more conical as opposed to cylindrical bore. Cite two examples of each.

   c. Describe a situation to be avoided in writing for trombone and how the F attachment affects the problem.

   d. Describe the baritone: its range compared to the tenor trombone, the number of valves the modern instrument has, and the various clefs and transpositions that may be used in the parts.

   e. When were valves introduced to brass instruments? How did they change the capacities of the previous "natural" instruments?

   f. Explain how mutes affect the sound of brass instruments, and describe three different types of mutes. What concerns are there when calling for their use?

Chapter Five

Percussion Instruments

Do not over-use

Percussion instruments, which produce a sound when they are struck, shaken, or scraped, fall into two broad categories: indefinite pitch and definite pitch. Timpani appears on the orchestral score above indefinite pitch instruments such as drums and cymbals. Last are instruments of definite pitch such as orchestra bells, xylophone, and celesta. The indefinite pitch instruments are often notated on a single line rather than on a staff. Most orchestras have at least three percussionists available, and several instruments may be notated in a single part if they are not played simultaneously. The number of players, instruments, tunings, and special directions must be indicated at the beginning of the score and parts. Many times the most effective percussion part consists of a small score for the entire section, excluding timpani, showing how all the instruments interact. This arrangement allows players to use their individual strengths and provides cues for entry.

The percussion section is used primarily in two ways: (1) for melodic or thematic purposes, where the pitched instruments such as timpani and mallets are most useful, and (2) to provide coloration and special effects, where unpitched instruments like the triangle, cymbals, or tambourine might be used. The dynamic range of the percussion section can be greater at both extremes than all the rest of the instruments in the orchestra combined, so very careful directions regarding volume and intensity must be included.

Logistics are a prime consideration when dealing with percussion. If several instruments played at different times in the music can be handled by one performer, include literal directions in the part well in advance of each change. Be sure to allow the performer time to place cymbals on their stands or walk around the timpani. In short, anticipate every movement the percussionist must make when constructing the part. Large notation and clearly written directions are important because these players are not often stationary and must look away from the music frequently.

BASIC PERCUSSION STROKES

Single stroke: the basic gesture of striking an object once, setting up vibrations. Combinations of strokes, or ornamented notes, are particularly common in snare drum writing. Occurring slightly before the beat, these ornaments are used to broaden the sound. They are notated as follows:

(a.)   (b.)   (c.)   (d.)   (e.)

Most no clef or key signature but must have meter

FIGURE 5.1   *Ornaments and rolls: (a) flam, (b) ruff, (c) four-stroke ruff, (d) roll, (e) roll with even division of the beat*

Flam: a rapid combination of two single strokes, one played by each hand.

Three-stroke ruff: a rapid combination of three strokes, most often L-L-R or R-R-L; the term "drag" is also used.

Four-stroke ruff: four rapid strokes, L-L-L-R, R-R-R-L, or alternating sticks.

Roll: rapid alternating strokes; any time mallets are used, a single-stroke roll is executed.

> *Open roll* (rudimental roll): consists of a stroke and a single rebound; used primarily by marching band snare drums.

> *Concert roll* (closed, multibounce, or press roll): consists of a stroke and two or three rebounds, creating a sustained effect. This is normally the type of roll executed by orchestral snare drummers.

The trill symbol should not be used to specify a roll, because it specifies the alternation between two different pitches. Note values included in a roll are tied to avoid undesired accents. A roll between two instruments is notated as a tremolo.

FIGURE 5.2   *Examples of tremolo between two timpani*

Dead sticking: stick does not rebound but remains in contact with the surface.

Rim shot (stick shot): one stick strikes the other, which is held with the tip on the center of the head, and the side of stick on the rim. In an alternate method, the stick strikes down on the head and rim simultaneously. Both sound like the crack of a pistol and are notated with the letters "RS" over the note head.

When notating duration for instruments with little natural sustain, use convenient and easy-to-read note values, as with pizzicato notation for strings. For instruments with more sustain, such as cymbals, indicate precise durations. The letters "l.v." (let vibrate) instruct the performer not to dampen the sound. Another way to indicate that the sound is not dampened is to use a tie extending into space to the right of the note that sustains. Orchestrators should be specific in their notation of rolls for mallet performers on the xylophone and marimba and not assume that long note values will automatically be rolled.

The force of the stroke, point of impact, and material with which the instrument is struck all play a part in the kind of sound produced. Special instructions in this regard should be placed in the score and parts. The following is a listing of various striking implements and their symbols. The harder the implement, the sharper the attack.

Snare drum stick   Triangle beater   Wire brush

Rubber/plastic mallet   Wooden mallet   Yarn mallet

FIGURE 5.3 *Symbols for beaters*

It is important to indicate where on the instrument the mallet or stick is to strike. The center of a drumhead produces a dead sound when struck; hitting nearer the edge produces a full, more normal sound. Dynamics and timbre vary widely from the center to the edge of any stretched membrane.

IT: *timpani*   FR: *timbales*   GER: *Pauken*

Timpani   timbales   Pauken

PROPERTIES   Also called kettle drums, the timpani has a parabolic body of copper alloy or fiberglass. A calfskin or plastic head is stretched over a metal hoop, which is fastened to the top of the drum by metal tuning screws. These screws are connected to a pedal mechanism. Pressing the pedal down increases the tension and raises the pitch.

RANGE BY DRUM SIZE

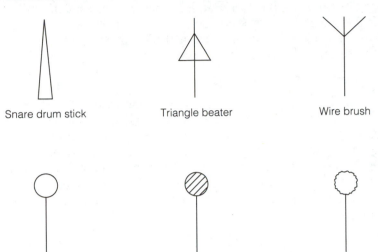

30"   28"   25"   23"

FIGURE 5.4   *Timpani range by drum size*

P.R
+ 8ve ? ↑
↓

It   FR   Ger
timpani   timbales   Pauken
timpani   timbales   Pauken
*   timbales   Pauken*
*   timbales   Pauken*
*   timbales   Pauken*
*   Pauken*

middle range
best for all timpani drums
don't hop around on timpani

Bass clef — regular notes use

function
Harmonic support
3 timpani used for I IV V
and one left over to use for the most harmonic/ note used

TRANSPOSITION   The timpani sounds as written. The compass of each drum is approximately a perfect fifth up from its lowest note. Notate the tuning pitch in bass clef for each drum at the beginning of the score and part.

TONE QUALITY   Resonance is best when the drum is struck about a third of the way from the rim to the center. Drum tuning is a critical factor in the tone. At the bottom of its range each drum sounds flabby and unfocused. At the top of its range, with the membrane stretched tightly, a thin sound with a "ping" results. The tone sustains unless it is dampened by the hand. Where pitch is important, double with other bass instruments. A pedal point is possible without the doubling.

TECHNICAL ABILITIES   Single notes, rhythmic figures, and rolls are all effective. Tremolo rolls between two drums are common. Glissando is accomplished by depressing the pedal while the note sounds. When pitch changes are necessary for the timpani, allow sufficient time for the player to make changes and test the new tuning. Three or four measures at a moderate tempo should be adequate time. Tuning gauges have become a popular accessory because they facilitate rapid changes and also aid beginning students. Tuning changes are indicated in the following way:

Change G to G♭

It: *G muta in G♭*   Fr: *changez sol en sol♭*   Ger: *G nach Ges umstimmen*

INDEFINITE PITCH INSTRUMENTS → rhythmic enhansment and shpport

BASS DRUM

It: *gran cassa*   Fr: *grosse caisse*   Ger: *grosse Trommel*
gran cassa   grosse caisse   gross Trommel

usually used with snare drums and cymbals

PROPERTIES   This drum is two-headed and cylindrical, approximately 16 inches deep and 32 to 36 inches in diameter. Although it is usually played with a lamb's wool beater, any kind of beater may be used. Response is slow, and simple rhythms with single strokes are recommended. A roll can create a thunderous effect. Avoid writing strong accents on regular beats unless the image of a parade is desired.

CYMBALS

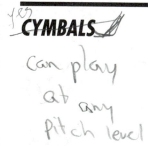

Can play at any pitch level

CRASH CYMBALS
It: *piatti, cinelli*   Fr: *cymbales*   Ger: *Becken*
Piatti, cinelli   cymbales   Becken

PROPERTIES   Usually 17 to 22 inches in diameter, cymbals are held in each hand by the strap attached to the center. They are brushed or clashed together and allowed to ring.

IT: *piatto sospeso*   FR: *cymbale suspendue*   GER: *Hängendes Becken*

Creates a sense of mystery and can be used to create a Climax.

PROPERTIES   Suspended cymbals typically are in three sizes: small (10–14 inches), medium (15–18 inches), and large (19–24 inches). They have a wide dynamic range and may be struck with any type mallet or stick. Struck at the edge, they produce a rich, bright sound; struck near the bell, they have a dull, gonglike sound. Rolls with soft mallets are effective, as are single strokes. Ordinary note heads and values are the preferred notation, rather than the "X" with a stem seen in some scores. Short notes are accomplished by choking the sound with the hand. The term "laissez vibrer" (or l.v.) is used to indicate free vibration, and the term "sec" is used to indicate the choked effect.

IT: *tamburo militare*   FR: *tambour militaire*   GER: *Militärtrommel*

PROPERTIES   Played with wooden sticks, this two-headed cylindrical drum with wire or gut snares stretched across the bottom rests horizontally on a stand. Dimensions are typically 5 to 8 inches in depth with a 14-inch diameter. The snares may be taut or loose; the drum resembles a tom-tom with the snares loosened. Unless the direction "snares off" is used, the normal manner of performance is with the snares on. This instrument was formerly referred to as a side drum.

EFFECTS   Two of the most effective applications of the snare drum are to highlight rhythmic accents and to augment a crescendo with a roll. Head tension may be adjusted for crisp (taut) or muffled (loose) sounds. Wire brushes are used in some styles of playing. The rim shot is particularly effective.

IT: *tamburo rullante*   FR: *caisse roulante*   GER: *Rührtrommel*

no snare

PROPERTIES   This drum is larger than the snare, varying in diameter from 10 to 12 inches and in depth from 14 to 17 inches. It has no snares. It is usually played with hard felt mallets, but snare drum sticks may be used for a more precise sound.

IT: *tamburo*   FR: *caisse sourde*   GER: *Jazzpauke*

PROPERTIES   These drums may have one or two heads and are cylindrical, much like tenor drums. Various sizes are often combined. Dimensions are typically 12 to 18 inches in diameter and 8 to 20 inches in depth. Tom-toms have no snares and are played with either sticks or mallets.

TAMBOURINE

IT: *tamburino*   FR: *tambour de Basque*   GER: *Schellentrommel*

PROPERTIES   The tambourine is a small wooden hoop about 10 inches in diameter with a calfskin head and jingles on the sides. It is commonly struck with the fist, palm, or sticks; it may also be shaken. Thumb rolls, produced by rubbing the thumb around the head near the rim, are advisable for low dynamic levels only. A shake roll is better for long durations and wide dynamic variation.

It
tamburino
tamburino
tamburino
tamburino
tamburino

FR →
tambour de Ba

TRIANGLE

IT: *triangolo*   FR: *triangle*   GER: *Triangel*

PROPERTIES   The triangle is a metal bar bent into a triangular shape, usually from 6 to 10 inches on a side. It is typically held by a cord suspended from the hand used to dampen it. Struck with a metal triangle beater, it has a wide dynamic range and a complex overtone structure.

TAM-TAM

or
Gong

Spelled the same in all languages, the tam-tam is a large circular piece of metal suspended from a frame, something like a flattened bell. A similar instrument of fixed pitch is called a gong, although the terms are used interchangeably.

OTHER PERCUSSION OF INDEFINITE PITCH

This category also includes wood block, Chinese temple blocks, claves, timbales, hi-hat cymbals, finger cymbals, drums, sleigh bells, guiro, maracas, conga, anvil, jaw bone, and bull roar.

DEFINITE PITCH INSTRUMENTS – *melodic instruments*

XYLOPHONE *FR.*

melodic
instrument

IT: *silofono*   FR: *xylophon*   GER: *Xylophon*

PROPERTIES   The xylophone has hardwood bars arrayed like a keyboard, with or without a resonator below each bar. Its brittle, incisive tone decays immediately, but may be sustained with a roll. Usually played with hard mallets, it can penetrate thick orchestral textures. The xylophone is frequently used to highlight melodic lines in unison with other instruments, particularly on rapid figures.

RANGE

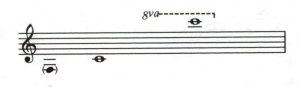

FIGURE 5.5 *Xylophone range*

TRANSPOSITION   The xylophone sounds an octave above the written pitch and is notated in treble clef. The low end of the range varies on different instruments. A safe compass is from c¹ upwards three octaves, although most college and professional organizations will have a larger instrument with the f below c¹ available.

The celesta is spelled the same in all languages.

PROPERTIES   The celesta resembles a very small spinet piano in appearance. It has a shorter keyboard and a damper pedal only. Instead of strings, the hammers strike small steel plates, each with a wooden resonator. The tone is bell-like, delicate, and not brilliant. It is used primarily to highlight melodies in soft passages. The technique is similar to that of the piano. The celesta sounds an octave higher than written.

RANGE

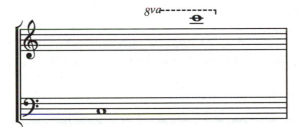

FIGURE 5.6 *Celesta range*

IT: *campanelli*   FR: *jeu de timbres, carillon*   GER: *Glockenspiel*

PROPERTIES   Metal bars arranged in the shape of a keyboard are attached to a portable case, which is opened and placed on a table in performance. Usually played with one or two hard mallets, the bells add a bright edge to the sound when combined with other instruments. The color is so distinctive it should be used with discretion.

RANGE

FIGURE 5.7 *Orchestra bells range*

TRANSPOSITION   The orchestra bells sound two octaves higher than written and are notated in the treble clef. The compass is from g upwards two octaves and a perfect fourth.

TUBULAR BELLS OR CHIMES
P. R.

IT: *campane*   FR: *tubes de cloches*   GER: *Röhrenglocken*

PROPERTIES   Tubular bells consist of a set of metal tubes 40 to 60 inches in length, closed at the top, and hung vertically in two rows. They are equipped with a damper that is operated by the foot, and a rawhide mallet is normally used to strike them. The actual pitch is obscure, and the sound is similar to church bells.

RANGE

FIGURE 5.8   *Tubular bells range*

TRANSPOSITION   Tubular bells sound as written and are notated in the treble clef. The compass is from c¹ upwards one octave and a perfect fourth.

MARIMBA P. R.

could be
a solo
instruments

Marimba is spelled the same in all languages.

PROPERTIES   The marimba is similar to the xylophone but is larger and has resonators. The softer wooden bars produce a mellow effect, creating a sound that is easily absorbed by other instruments in its middle and low ranges. It can become quite bright in the upper range with hard mallets. The marimba is usually played with yarn or soft rubber mallets, but soft cord mallets are used to good effect throughout the range.

RANGE

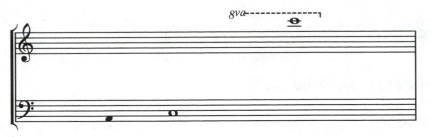

FIGURE 5.9   *Marimba range*

TRANSPOSITION   The marimba sounds as written and is commonly notated on a grand staff like the piano. The compass is from c upwards four octaves on most instruments, but most new models include the low A.

IT: *vibrafono*   FR: *vibraphone*   GER: *Vibraphon*

PROPERTIES   Two rows of steel bars arranged like a keyboard are suspended over resonating tubes. Small discs are turned inside the resonators by an electric motor, producing a vibrato of adjustable speed. (Indicate "fan off" to stop the vibrato.) A damper pedal similar to that of a piano is employed, and vibe parts should be marked accordingly. Usually played with soft or medium mallets, it produces a mellow sound, bright in the high register, that blends well with the upper woodwinds. The instrument was developed for the jazz idiom in the 1920s, is an accepted member of the band, and is also used in late twentieth century orchestral scores.

RANGE

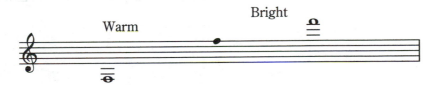

FIGURE 5.10   *Vibraphone range*

TRANSPOSITION   The vibes sound as written and are notated in treble clef or grand staff. The compass is from f upwards three octaves.

IT: *crotales*   FR: *crotales*   GER: *antike Zimbeln*

PROPERTIES   These are thick brass plates, 2 to 5 inches in diameter, usually mounted on a rack or suspended. They are struck with a brass mallet. If pairs are used, they are struck together lightly. The soft bell-like sound produced blends with high-register strings, woodwinds, and harp.

RANGE

FIGURE 5.11   *Antique cymbals range*

TRANSPOSITION   Notated in treble clef, the sound is one octave higher than written pitch. A set of thirteen covering the octave c^2–c^3 is common.

ROTO-TOMS

Roto-toms are tunable drums made in various sizes. They have no resonators and consist of a metal frame over which the plastic head is stretched. Rotating the drum on its base tightens or loosens the head, which in turn raises or lowers the pitch. Range of each drum according to size is listed below.

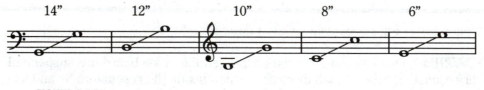

FIGURE 5.12   *Roto-tom ranges*

As with timpani, indicate tuning of drums at the beginning of the score. Any type of stick or mallet may be used.

OTHER PERCUSSION OF DEFINITE PITCH

This category includes steel drums, hand bells, musical glasses, and flexatone.

MUSICAL EXAMPLE

FIGURE 5.13 Rimsky-Korsakov, Capriccio Espagnol, Op. 34, V., Fandango asturiano, measures 1–4. Can you give the English name for each instrument used?

EXERCISES FOR PERCUSSION SCORING

1. Add parts for two timpani, snare drum, bass drum, and orchestra bells to the score.

March tempo

F and A 2 Timp.

Snare

Bass

Bells

2. Give English equivalents for the following:

a. Tam-Tam

b. Pauken

c. Crotali

d. Piatti

e. Campanelli

f. Gran cassa

g. Tamburo

h. Becken

For Project

Picc

I, II Flute

I, II Oboe

I, II Bb Clarinet

I, II Bassoon

4 Horns

2 Trumpets (Bb)

I, II Trombone

III, Tuba
Tromb.

3 percussion (at least one mallet)

I, II Violin

Viola

Cello

Bass

Exam: Terms

+ we need to have ok for final project.

3. Indicate True (T) or False (F):

a. _____ The order of percussion in a score from top to bottom is (1) indefinite pitch, (2) definite pitch, (3) timpani.

b. _____ The extremes of dynamic range are greater for the percussion than for the other orchestral sections combined.

c. _____ The xylophone has metal bars arranged like the piano keyboard.

d. _____ The type of beater or mallet used has very little effect on the sound produced by percussion instruments.

e. _____ The triangle, tambourine, and claves are instruments of indefinite pitch.

4. Notate the following percussion techniques.

a. four-stroke ruff on the third beat

$\dfrac{4}{4}$

b. roll for 5 beats (unmeasured)

$\dfrac{4}{4}$

c. unstopped cymbal crash on the 4th beat

$\dfrac{4}{4}$

Chapter Six

Other Instruments

IT: *arpa*   FR: *harpe*   GER: *Harfe*

PROPERTIES   The modern double-action harp has forty-seven strings that are attached at a 45° angle to the soundboard. The strings are white except for the red C strings and the purple F strings. The double-action harp rests on a pedestal that houses seven foot pedals. A column rising from the pedestal supports the neck, which curves downward to the hollow back, or soundboard, and contains the tuning pegs. The strings are stretched between the neck and the soundboard. The harp part is written on a grand staff, and the instrument is nontransposing.

RANGE

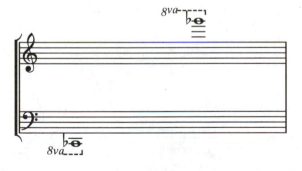

FIGURE 6.1   Harp range with pedals in the upper position

PEDAL POSITIONS

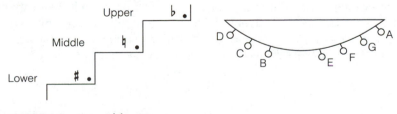

FIGURE 6.2   Harp pedal positions

TUNING The harp is tuned to a C♭ major scale with all the pedals in the upper position. Each pedal controls all strings of the same pitch in their different octaves and has three positions. The note is flatted in the upper position and is raised a semitone, becoming a natural, in the middle position. In the lowest position the note is raised another semitone, producing a sharp.

(a) $\begin{bmatrix} E^\flat & F^\sharp & G & A \\ B^\flat & C & D \end{bmatrix}$ (b)

FIGURE 6.3   Harp tunings: (a) string tuning and (b) pedal positions

PEDAL NOTATIONS Figure 6.2 shows the location of the pedals on the harp and the pitches they control. Figure 6.3 shows two methods of indicating to the harpist how the pedals are to be positioned and the strings tuned for each section of the music. All natural pitches are in the middle position; all sharps are in the lowest position. Tunings involving as many flats as possible are the most desirable, with the strings vibrating at their full length. The low CC, and on some harps the DD, are not connected to the pedal and cannot be changed during performance. Two pedals can be moved at once if they are on opposite sides of the instrument, and a sequence of pedal changes can be done relatively rapidly. Orchestrators should avoid requiring frequent pedal changes for beginning and intermediate players.

TECHNICAL ABILITIES The fingers are numbered from thumb (1) to annular (4). Stretches between fingers vary according to the size of the performer's hand. Generally, fingers 1 and 2 reach the interval of a fourth, 1 to 3 reach a fifth or sixth, and 1 to 4 reach an octave. The little finger is not used. Difficulties for the performer increase when parts require the hands to be too close together or too far apart (at opposite ends of the instrument). Chords and arpeggios are the most common figures. The glissando is a very effective device, although it can become a cliché. The following are examples of these harp techniques:

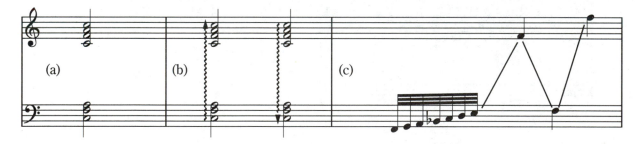

FIGURE 6.4   Harp techniques: (a) block chord, (b) arpeggio (up and down), (c) glissando

The harp does not penetrate a thick orchestral texture, but it has a very sharp staccato in the upper two octaves and good resonance in the lower two. Harmonics are easily sounded on most strings by dividing them in half with light pressure. The harp is used effectively to accent the beginning of a phrase with other instruments, particularly strings. Compositions such as Debussy's *La Mer* (see Appendix B) and Ravel's *Daphne et Chloe* utilize the harp effectively.

IT: *chitarra*   FR: *guitare*   GER: *Gitarre*

PROPERTIES   The classical guitar has six strings made of nylon, the lower of which are wound with metal. There are frets embedded in the neck, spaced so that the distance between adjacent frets is a half-step on any string. A finger of the left hand presses the string beside the fret slightly toward the nut to stop its vibrations at the fret. The thumbnail and fingernails of the right hand are used to pluck the strings.

TUNING AND RANGE

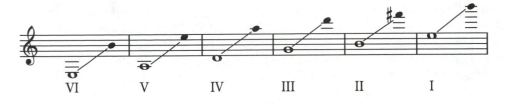

VI   V   IV   III   II   I

FIGURE 6.5   *Guitar tuning and range*

TRANSPOSITION   The guitar part is written in the treble clef and sounds an octave lower. There is an interval of a perfect fourth between each string except III and II, where the distance is a major third. The sound of the classical guitar is delicate and very easily covered.

TECHNICAL ABILITIES   Sharp keys, more easily negotiated on the guitar than flat keys, allow the use of more open strings and sympathetic vibrations. Chords should be written with no more than a fifth or sixth between notes. The first finger of the left hand may be used to stop all or some of the strings at a given fret. This technique is called the grande barre, or simply barre.

NOTATION   If a note is to be played on a particluar string, the number of that string (1–6) is placed beside the note and circled. If a particular finger of the left hand is to be used, the number of the finger (1–4) is placed by the note, and the finger number is not circled. The circle around the number differentiates the string from the finger identified. The left thumb is not used. Lowercase alphabet letters are used to indicate which finger of the right hand should be used to pluck the string.

Left Hand		Right Hand
1	index finger	i
2	middle finger	m
3	annular (ring) finger	a
4	small (little) finger	s
not used	thumb	p

CHORD DIAGRAMS   Though they are not a part of formal classical guitar notation, chord diagrams representing the position of the fingers on the frets are common in many guitar styles. These indicate the first five frets from the nut, with fingers numbered in their position on the string. Open strings have an "o" over them, and deadened or unused strings are marked with an "x." A bar is represented by a curved line over the position where all strings are depressed by the first finger.

The following are examples of standard chord diagrams and their equivalents in musical notation:

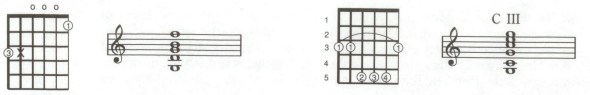

FIGURE 6.6 *Guitar chord diagrams*

EFFECTS AND FIGURATIONS   Harmonics of open strings are easily produced by lightly touching the strings at frets XII, VII, and V.   Arpeggiation of chords is perhaps the most common figure occurring in guitar music. The term "tremolo" in reference to guitar technique means to pluck the same string rapidly with different fingers of the right hand.

FIGURE 6.7   *Guitar tremolo*

PIANO

IT: *pianoforte*   FR: *piano*   GER: *Klavier*

PROPERTIES   The metal strings of the piano are stretched on a cast iron frame parallel to the soundboard. Vertical pianos ascend in height from small spinets to studio uprights, which accommodate strings as long as a small grand piano. Grand pianos are horizontal and vary in length from the baby grand (under 5 feet long) to the concert grand (11 feet long). When a piano key is depressed, the damper, which rests on the string, is raised, and a felt hammer strikes the string. There are no dampers in the upper register. In the lowest range there is one string for each note, in the middle to lower ranges, two strings, and in the middle to high range three strings for each note.

RANGE

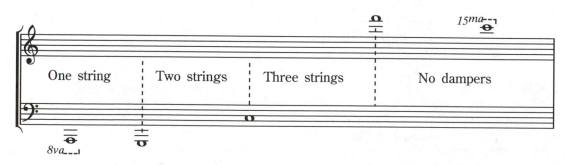

FIGURE 6.8   *Piano range. The points at which the number of strings changes will vary on different pianos, so an average is shown here.*

PEDALS All pianos are equipped with a damper pedal on the right that raises all dampers from the strings when it is depressed. The una corda pedal on the left shifts the action of the grand piano so that the hammer strikes only one string in the middle range and two strings in the high range. Most grand pianos have a sostenuto pedal located between the other two. If the sostenuto pedal is lowered while keys are depressed, the dampers over those strings will remain raised until the pedal is released. Pedal indications are shown below.

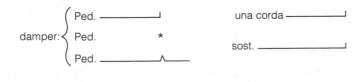

FIGURE 6.9 *Piano pedal indications*

TONE QUALITY Because the tone of the piano has very little sustaining power but a strong accent, it is often used in a percussive capacity in the orchestra. The lowest notes are gonglike and the highest pitches bell-like and undampened. An extremely wide dynamic range is available from the grand piano.

TECHNIQUE The piano has few technical limitations. Rapid scales, arpeggios, leaps, tremolo, and trills are possible. Both hands may be used together in the treble or bass regions, or the hands may cross. Block chords should be voiced within an octave or a ninth for each hand. A wide space between intervals in full chords may exist between the thumb and first finger of each hand. Spaces between adjacent fingers should be narrower.

DEVELOPING AN ACCOMPANIMENT

The instruments discussed in this chapter all have the capacity to perform chords, or simultaneous combinations of pitches. They are often selected by the orchestrator to provide a harmonic and rhythmic accompaniment to solo winds, strings, and voices. They can also be used to support their own melodies, providing both the primary line and background figures. A wide range of accompanimental techniques can be employed with these chordal instruments. In homophonic music with a single line melody and a chordal background, patterns that provide a harmonic context for the melody and also establish the degree of rhythmic activity can be devised. Common figures for the chordal instrument in this capacity are created in the following ways:

1. Arpeggiate the chords upwards or downwards, where the lowest note becomes the bass, and the figure remains constant in its shape. The alberti bass is an example of this type of figure.

2. Alternate single bass notes with block chords. This common figure is used in the waltz and in marching band music. Syncopating the rhythm between the bass and chords creates a ragtime effect.

3. A tremolo figure alternating between two different pitches is a useful device that provides some density. The two pitches must be chosen carefully to elucidate the harmonic content most clearly.

4. A combination of arpeggiated and tremolo figures can be used. A particularly effective device is imitating fragments of the melodic line in the accompanimental part, which integrates the two functions and creates new expectations for the listener.

5. Repeating block chords in a regular pulse or rhythmic pattern is a good way to heighten the forward progress to points of arrival and lend power to the overall texture.

6. Long sustained chords, quietly rolled or arpeggiated, can provide a serene background to prepare the entry of a solo instrument.

There are many other possibilities, and the best accompaniments use a combination of figures and devices to enhance the musical flow. The character of the music and the ranges of the instruments used are both critical factors in determining the most suitable choices. In general, it is better to understate the accompaniment than to build an overly active texture that competes with primary melodic material.

For practice in applying the information in this chapter, select a melody, and harmonize it with an original accompaniment for harp, guitar, or piano. Perform your arrangement with a solo voice or instrument and the accompaniment.

Chapter Seven

Scoring for the Orchestra

Detailed information regarding the capabilities of instruments has been offered to this point to ensure that each part is practical to play, that awkward technical difficulties are avoided, and that the notation and transpositions are correct. Information regarding the tone qualities of the instruments in the various ranges is valuable in anticipating the ensemble blend. A quality that all successful orchestrators share is a well-developed aural imagination. Listening to recordings of a wide variety of music and analyzing scores are excellent ways to improve timbral conception. However, attending a live performance gives a much clearer impression of the real effects of scoring techniques than does listening to a recording. Performing in ensembles and attending rehearsals can be educational for the orchestration student if the ear is focused on the texture. One of the best ways to learn about scoring is to transcribe music for an available ensemble and to observe the performance.

TRANSCRIPTION

Transcription is the art of scoring music for instruments other than those designated in the original composition. A successful transcription, which captures the musical ideas and the spirit of the original work faithfully, requires that the arranger understand the piece thoroughly. A good understanding of the medium for which the transcription is intended is also necessary. Often the most important element is translating idiomatic figures for an ensemble other than the original with a comfortable, playable result. An initial practical consideration must be whether the original key is suitable or if a transposition would put the new ensemble in a more easily negotiated key. Determine the tessitura and range of the piece, and compare it to the capacities of the instruments to be used. Piano literature provides a wealth of suitable material for transcription; there are many ways to translate pianistic devices for orchestral textures.

As noted in Chapter Six, the piano often executes a rhythmic succession of notes outlining the harmony. This is chiefly due to the rapid decay of its tone. To a certain degree, performers can compensate for this by using the damper pedal. Low tones, usually harmonic roots, are frequently sustained by the pedal while upper harmonies are arpeggiated. This technique, along with alberti bass and tremolo patterns, are common means by which a piano sustains harmonies. Take into account pedal markings when transcribing note values, and lengthen notes in the transcription accordingly.

The pianistic texture can be replaced by more natural figures for a combination of monophonic instruments in many ways. Depending on the context, it will be necessary in the transcription to apply a judicious combination of sustained tones, repeated notes, and partial arpeggiations. It will often be beneficial to respace vertical sonorities if low pitches are grouped closely together in piano music. When assigning low harmonies to winds, wider intervals in the bass regions are preferable. Close voicing for wind sections is recommended in the upper register to avoid isolation and undesirable exposure of the top voice. Harmonies need to be filled in without leaving the large gaps often found in piano music. Be certain to identify the harmonic content, and be aware of which scale degrees are doubled. Keep subordinate figures in the background. The strings are well suited for all types of accompanimental duties, with wind instruments or first violins given the melody. Tremolo and broken octave figures work well with string combinations. Octave transposition may be applied to a line to place it in a suitable range on the instrument by which it is played.

Examples of original piano versions of a composition orchestrated by the composer offer a good insight into how to preserve the musical content while switching media. Some of these include:

1.   Brahms, *Hungarian Dance No. 1* (four hands originally) and *Variations on a Theme by Haydn* (two pianos originally)

2.   Dvořák, Slavonic Dances (four hands originally)

3.   Ravel, *Pavane pour une Infante Defunte* (two hands originally)

4.   Copland, Orchestral Variations (Piano Variations originally)

Transcriptions were commonplace in the nineteenth century. Liszt transcribed all of Beethoven's symphonies for piano. One of the most famous and effective twentieth-century transcriptions is Ravel's orchestration of Mussorgsky's *Pictures at an Exhibition*. Another exemplary transcription is Schoenberg's orchestral setting of the Brahms Piano Quartet in G minor. A master at transcription, and also at making borrowed material fit his purposes, was Igor Stravinsky. His transcriptions cross style periods and draw from a wide range of original media.

Music written for organ does not always present the idiomatic problems often associated with piano music. Registration indications in organ music are analogous to orchestration decisions. Concert pitch is represented by eight-foot stops, the octave above by four-foot stops, and the octave below by sixteen-foot stops. Diverse color combinations are possible, and organ manuals are utilized in the same way that choirs of instruments are utilized in the ensemble. Identify the role of the pedal in the composition, and preserve its function in transcription. Transferring musical ideas from one medium to another necessitates understanding the basic nature of the original sound. Although both string and vocal literature can be set for winds, homogeneous groups of instruments will be needed to achieve the high degree of blend found in the original.

PRIMARY AND SECONDARY LINES

Clear linear motion is an important element in polyphonic music. In most orchestral music vertical sonorities are the result of several lines heard simultaneously, and the forward linear movement creates the harmony. Primary lines must be distinguished from subordinate lines and orchestrated in a more prominent fashion. Important melodic lines can either be assigned to instruments with more vivid tone colors and penetrating power or placed above other pitches in the harmony. Because they are the most distinguishable to the ear, the top and bottom lines are of principal importance.

In highly contrapuntal music each part must maintain independence from the others, and preserving the clarity of each line is the primary concern in scoring. Arranging a fugue by J. S. Bach for a mixed chamber ensemble is an excellent exercise for applying techniques that help preserve linear independence, including the following:

1.   Assign single instruments of dissimilar tone color to each part, and keep the texture thin.

2.   Use octave transposition to prevent lines from overlapping too much in the same register, or double lines in different octaves.

3.   Apply both of these techniques, using contrasting choirs of similar instruments on different parts.

4.   Mark articulations very carefully so that the entry of a new part is a noticeable event in the texture. Marking each entry of the same subject with identical articulations greatly enhances the effect of imitation and saves rehearsal time.

5.   Use dynamic markings consistently with crescendos and diminuendos to control the intensity of each part. This helps the players identify their roles.

6.   In dense textures new entries may be highlighted with pitched percussion. This technique brings them to the foreground without adding mass.

7.   Another way to differentiate motives or themes from surrounding lines is to use short note values in one part and sustained tones in another part. This is especially applicable when combining two or more of the same instrument with different musical functions.

There are numerous ways of differentiating between the importance of lines in a composition, including the following:

1.   Assigning the prominent line to a single instrument with a distinct timbre is the simplest and one of the most effective ways of differentiating it from the background.

2.   Doubling with the same instrument at the unison can create intonation problems, particularly with a unique timbre such as the oboe. This problem can be alleviated by using three or more of the same instrument on the line.

3.   Doubling at the octave with the same instrument creates an interesting new tone quality and does not pose such serious intonation problems. The effect is one of greater penetration rather than greater mass. The soprano line is more effective doubled one octave above; the bass line more effective one octave below. The latter is a standard procedure for cellos and string basses.

4. Two or more different instruments on a line, either in unison or at octaves, can create a most colorful sound. The flute, clarinet, horn, and bassoon blend well with most other instruments and are easily absorbed. The oboe and trumpet tend to assert their tones. The tuba adds considerable mass to any combination.

5. Woodwinds are usually placed above the brass in combination, where they strengthen the upper partials. Placed among the brass, they lessen the brilliance without adding strength or color.

6. Combinations of woodwinds and strings lend resonance and body to the string tone and soften the winds. Except for the horn, brass and strings do not blend well.

7. A section of strings playing together is not necessarily much more powerful than a single instrument, but it is richer due to the chorus effect. The upper strings in their highest register have the capacity to pierce any texture except the forte brass and percussion.

Subordinate lines need to be scored in a contrasting hue, or pale color, in a controllable range of the instruments assigned. Several options for scoring secondary lines follow:

1. A group of similar sounding instruments which are easily covered assigned to each subordinate line can provide an innocuous background. Second violins, violas, and cellos are frequently used in this capacity, as are the clarinet and bass clarinet. The number of performers lessens the degree of individuality and tends to average out the articulations.

2. A group of dissimilar instruments on the line in one or more octaves is slightly more noticeable, depending upon the blend of voices chosen.

3. Single instruments assigned to the accompanying lines with similar sonorities stand out even more, providing clarity.

4. Subordinate lines can be given to single instruments, each with a unique timbre, for the strongest effect. This is the most interesting, yet problematic, solution due to differences in balance and blend. Whenever blend is important, the range of the instrument is a critical factor. Placing an instrument in an extreme part of its range frequently prevents a good blend and introduces problems with intonation.

Constant bright color in the ensemble begins to wear on the ear, as does rich food on the palate. The double reeds have a unique and often strident tone, but are not powerful and assertive. One factor that makes an instrument stand out or attract attention is the amount of vibrato the performer uses. Because the flute and strings generally are played with considerable vibrato, they are noticeable in a texture. The following table differentiates between the strong voices in the orchestra and those easily covered.

Strongest	Relatively Strong	Easily Covered
Piccolo	Oboe	Viola
Trumpet	Bassoon	Flute—low register
Trombone	*Clarinet	Bass clarinet
Timpani	*Horn	Double bass
Orchestra bells	Tuba	Harp
*Violin	*Cello	Celesta

(* indicates upper part of the range)

Drastically terraced dynamics should not be used to compensate for improper balance. It is, however, important to give players a clue as to their role in the ensemble by including some dynamic marking at all times. Articulations and phrasing should also always be included. One means of giving the background less force or weight is to use notes of shorter duration.

The overtone series has traditionally been used as a model for spacing and doubling chord voicing, thus providing a balanced and stable chord. The upper partials appear in close position, with more distance between the lower tones. Of the first sixteen partials, five are roots, three are fifths, and two are thirds. Unless a unique, striking sonority is desired, avoid top-heavy or bottom-heavy chords, and place the majority of the instruments in the middle.

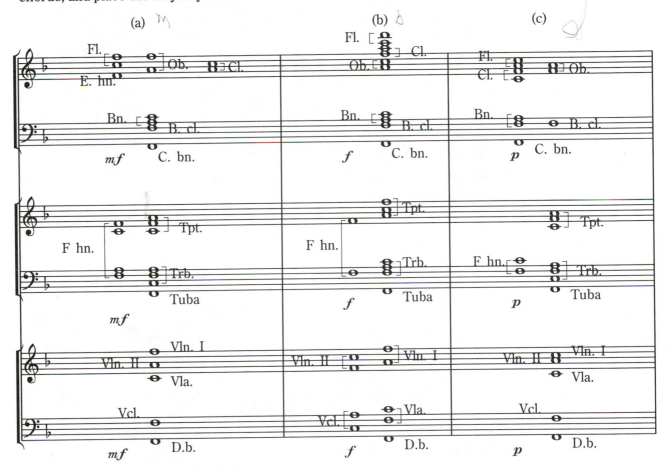

FIGURE 7.1   *Scoring chords for orchestra: (a) moderate, (b) bright, (c) dark*

Consider the sound space as though it were a landscape. There should be peaks and valleys, analogous to pitches in the extreme upper and lower ranges. Differentiate the foreground and background by varied tone colors, dynamics, and degrees of intensity. A good orchestration creates dimensions in the sound space in a manner that enhances the musical ideas presented.

Melody- Sop

I Violin / Fl / Ob / Cl / Tpt / Hn
       solo solo solo

Alto

II Vln / Viola / Ob / Cl / Hn / Tpt / Tbn

Tenor

Viola / Cello / Cl / BSN / Tbn / Hn

Bass

Cel / Bass / Bsn / Trombone / Tuba

Anything Can Solo

Strings	WW	Brass
I Vln	Flute	Tpt
II Vln	Oboe	Hn
Viola	Cl	Trombone
Cello	Bsn	Tuba
Bass		

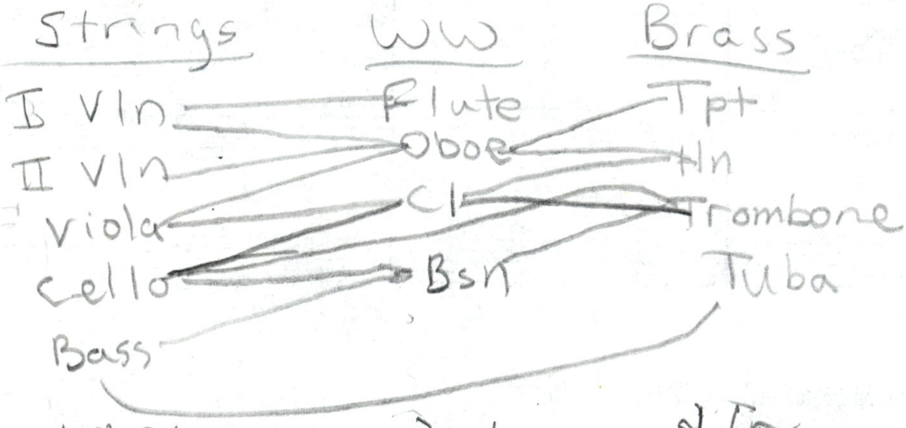

1 parts   2 pts   2 Tpt 1 staff
1 staff   1 staff   4 Hn 2 staffs
                            4 Trombones 1 staff
                            1 Tuba + 1 Trombone on 1 staff

Pg 90

EXERCISES FOR ORCHESTRAL SCORING

1. Transcribe the Chorale Prelude on *Christ lag in Todesbanden* by J. S. Bach for available instruments, and have it performed.

2. Score the chords for a small orchestra to achieve the sonorities requested.

3. Transcribe the excerpt from the Hugo Wolf song, "The Wandering Minstrel" for a mixed chamber ensemble.

4. *Review:* Number the following instruments as they would appear in order on an orchestral score. To the right of each place a W (woodwind), B (brass), P (percussion), or S (string).

a. ____ Bratsche ____

b. ____ Tromba ____

c. ____ Fagott ____

d. ____ Pauken ____

e. ____ Posaune ____

f. ____ Cor ____

g. ____ Piatti ____

h. ____ Hautbois ____

i. ____ Cor Anglais ____

j. ____ Bassklarinette ____

Chapter Eight

Orchestral Styles

A composer's orchestral style is the product of several factors. Because one determinant is the actual array of instruments available, the technology associated with instrument construction is of significance. Decisions regarding orchestration were based, of necessity, on the availability of instruments and performers. The first section of like instruments to emerge as a foundation of the orchestra was the string family. String ensembles were developed and refined in France through the middle of the seventeenth century by court musicians such as Lully. During the same period in Bologna, Italy, a large ensemble that included strings, winds, and organs was maintained at the basilica of San Petronio. Monteverdi's opera scores were among the most advanced of the period, containing some of the earliest indications for pizzicato and tremolo string techniques. Vivaldi's ensembles in Venice were influential in that they advanced the concerto concept and utilized the orchestra as an accompaniment. Torelli emigrated to Germany with his early symphonic style and eventually settled in Vienna, which became a center of orchestral activity.

In the later baroque period J. S. Bach demonstrated his contrapuntal style of scoring in the Brandenburg concerti. Handel helped to establish the customary practice of consistently combining double reeds, natural horns, military trumpets, and timpani with the string section. He is credited with three innovations: a part containing a solo for the bassoon, an orchestral score calling for four horns in 1724, and a timpani solo in 1739. In his early works the woodwinds were commonly doubled with the strings, as in the *Water Music*. In later scores, such as the *Royal Fireworks Music*, he contrasted the choirs of strings, double reeds, and brass. Around the same time Rameau was originating the French tendencies in orchestration, with a refined clarity typical of the style.

PRECLASSICIST

In the first half of the eighteenth century, public concerts became popular, and the size of the concert halls made new demands on instruments and performers alike. By 1750 instrumental music performed by large ensembles flourished in Paris, Frankfurt, Hamburg, and Vienna. Sammartini was developing symphonic forms in Milan. In addition to strings, he included horn parts and implied that a keyboard with a bass instrument be used for the continuo. He established a direction in musical form that Haydn would follow.

FIGURE 8.1 Historical Development of the Instruments

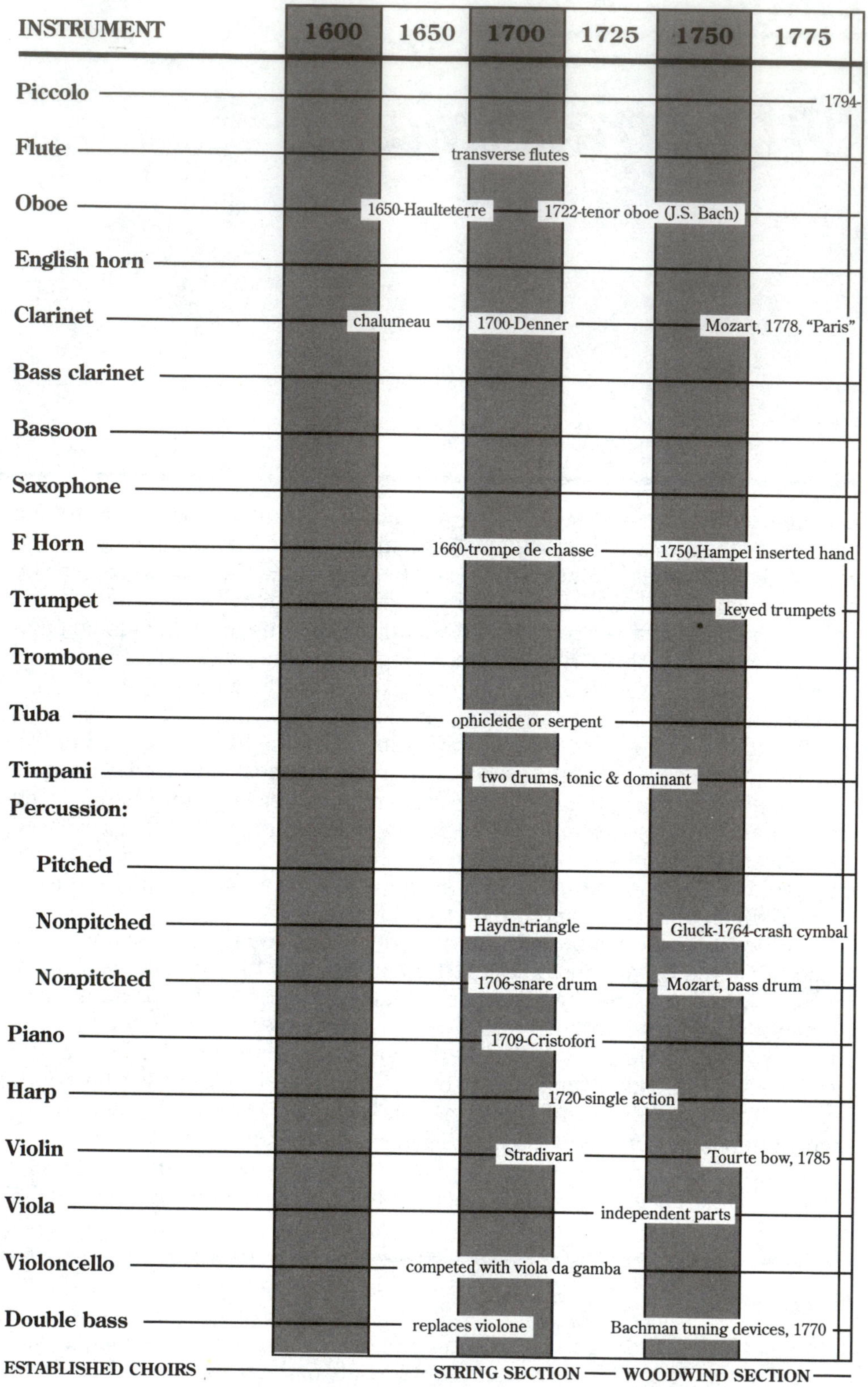

INSTRUMENT	1600	1650	1700	1725	1750	1775
Piccolo						1794-
Flute			transverse flutes			
Oboe		1650-Haulteterre		1722-tenor oboe (J.S. Bach)		
English horn						
Clarinet		chalumeau	1700-Denner		Mozart, 1778, "Paris"	
Bass clarinet						
Bassoon						
Saxophone						
F Horn			1660-trompe de chasse		1750-Hampel inserted hand	
Trumpet					keyed trumpets	
Trombone						
Tuba			ophicleide or serpent			
Timpani			two drums, tonic & dominant			
Percussion:						
Pitched						
Nonpitched			Haydn-triangle		Gluck-1764-crash cymbal	
Nonpitched			1706-snare drum		Mozart, bass drum	
Piano			1709-Cristofori			
Harp			1720-single action			
Violin			Stradivari		Tourte bow, 1785	
Viola				independent parts		
Violoncello		competed with viola da gamba				
Double bass		replaces violone		Bachman tuning devices, 1770		
ESTABLISHED CHOIRS			STRING SECTION		WOODWIND SECTION	

98

FIGURE 8.1 *Historical Development of the Instruments (continued)*

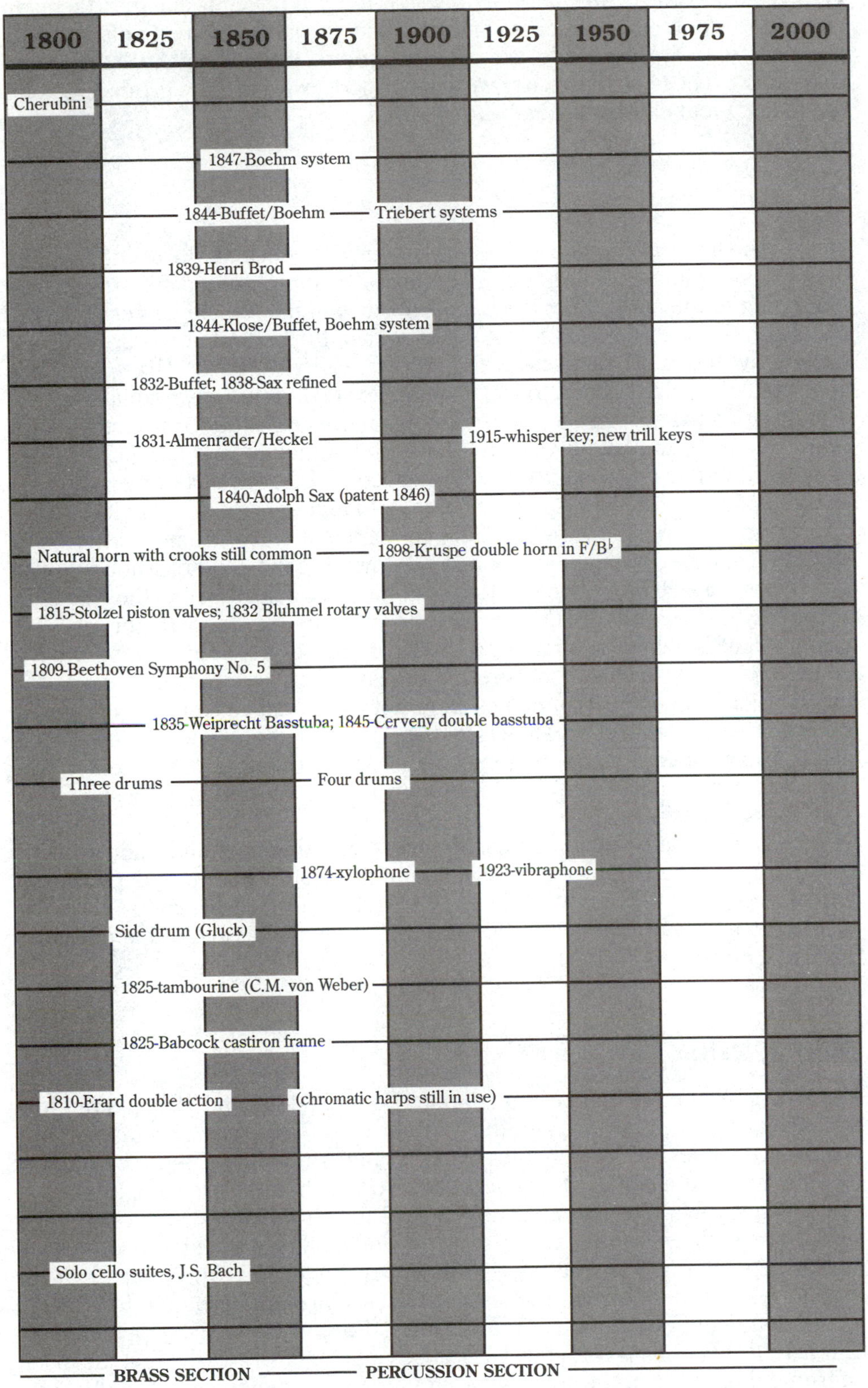

1800	1825	1850	1875	1900	1925	1950	1975	2000

Cherubini

1847-Boehm system

1844-Buffet/Boehm ——— Triebert systems

1839-Henri Brod

1844-Klose/Buffet, Boehm system

1832-Buffet; 1838-Sax refined

1831-Almenrader/Heckel ——— 1915-whisper key; new trill keys

1840-Adolph Sax (patent 1846)

Natural horn with crooks still common ——— 1898-Kruspe double horn in F/B♭

1815-Stolzel piston valves; 1832 Bluhmel rotary valves

1809-Beethoven Symphony No. 5

1835-Weiprecht Basstuba; 1845-Cerveny double basstuba

Three drums ——— Four drums

1874-xylophone   1923-vibraphone

Side drum (Gluck)

1825-tambourine (C.M. von Weber)

1825-Babcock castiron frame

1810-Erard double action ——— (chromatic harps still in use)

Solo cello suites, J.S. Bach

——— BRASS SECTION ——— PERCUSSION SECTION ———

Georg Monn of the Viennese school was influential, as was Wagenseil. In his preface to the *Denkmaler deutscher Tonkunst*, the musicologist Riemann cited the "Mannheim school" as an important group that helped define a symphonic style. Most notable among this group were Stamitz, Richter, and Cannabich. These preclassicists were key figures who laid the groundwork for the major Viennese composers who followed.

CLASSICAL

During the latter part of the eighteenth century, Haydn and Mozart defined the classical symphonic ideal. Haydn's resources centered around the strings, and beginning in the early 1770s the harpsichord continuo was no longer included. Haydn consciously wrote with the limitations of the natural horns in mind and frequently added a pair of natural trumpets, called "clarini." His woodwinds consisted of a pair of oboes, to which clarinets and flutes were gradually added. The bassoon parts became independent from those of other bass instruments. A pair of small timpani tuned to the tonic and dominant rounded out Haydn's orchestra. With a few notable exceptions, such as the contra bassoon part in the *Creation,* Haydn's style was conservative, with understated use of color.

Mozart wrote for much the same combination, but with more interesting techniques. One combination he often used was the flute and bassoon doubled two octaves apart with oboe or clarinet at a sixth or third below the flute. His string writing was more adventurous than that of Haydn, with the possible exception of Haydn's late masses. He utilized the clarinet in his Symphony No. 23 and frequently in chamber scores, but it did not have a clearly defined role in the classical orchestra. Trombones were not commonly used in the orchestra, except in sacred choral works, where they doubled alto, tenor, and bass vocal parts. Mozart also used them in his operas, as did Haydn in the *Creation.* The harp was almost never employed in the orchestra, and little percussion other than timpani was used.

During the late eighteenth century new instruments found their way into the opera pit, where more expressive, dramatic music was required. Gluck was an early pioneer of orchestral devices, utilizing the piccolo, contra bassoon, clarinet, trombone, English horn, and harp. A good example of his advanced style is *Iphigenie en Tauride*, composed in 1779.

EARLY ROMANTIC

Beethoven wrote his first six symphonies between 1799 and 1808, adding the seventh and eighth by 1812 and the ninth in 1824. These works remain monuments to which all symphonies before and after have been compared. Beethoven used a standard classical orchestra in the first two symphonies. In the seven symphonies that followed he gave the strings five distinct parts and used them in divisi fashion. His third, sixth, and ninth symphonies incorporated the piccolo, clarinet, and bassoon in its upper range. The *Eroica* was a major step forward in Beethoven's orchestral style. All through his output Beethoven wrote demanding parts for natural horns, and never used valved instruments, English horns, or bass clarinets. His Fifth Symphony marked the first inclusion of trombones in the orchestra. The programmatic characterizations in the Sixth Symphony were unique, and the massive vocal and instrumental forces in the Ninth Symphony foreshadowed later romantic tendencies.

Beethoven's contemporary, Schubert, was a competent yet modest orchestrator. His use of trombones in the second movement of the *Unfinished* Symphony was unusual at the time. Mendelssohn wrote with sensitivity for instruments, and the scherzo from his *Midsummer Night's Dream* shows delicate control of woodwind timbres. Schumann's scoring was very dense and full, and it worked well with the forces he had at his disposal.

Carl Maria von Weber showed great expressive capacity with instruments in his Overture to *Der Freischütz,* composed in 1820. He was a true revolutionary who standardized the use of four horns, two trumpets, and three trombones. Giacomo Meyerbeer also introduced new instruments in a striking and unusual fashion. He is credited with the first bass clarinet solo, as well as use of the English horn and harp.

Berlioz was a major contributor to the field and a strong romantic influence for whom orchestration was both the means and the end. His *Treatise on Instrumentation* was the first comprehensive work on the subject. His brass sections competed on an even footing with the woodwinds and strings. Even with the tuba, which he was among the first to include in the ensemble, his brass pianissimo was a trademark. The *Symphonie Fantastique* is a landmark example of ways in which instrumental colors can be cast.

The middle period romantics made several adjustments to the orchestra. The string sound developed with the advent of the concave Tourte bow, expanding in size to balance with increasing numbers of winds, with independent parts for each instrument and special effects. Composers at this time called for more woodwinds, added the piccolo, but still did not regularly employ the English horn or contra bassoon. They made use of the improved valved brass but were not in the habit of adding the tuba. The typical number of timpani grew to three, and more use was made of the bass drum, cymbals, triangle, and harp. Curiously, the convention of ordering the score by choirs was not consistently practiced by all composers in the middle romantic period.

LATE ROMANTIC

The symphony orchestra continued to grow in many ways through the late nineteenth century. The size of string sections expanded as the numbers of brass, woodwinds, and percussion increased. Sixty-five string players was a common number in a late romantic symphony. The four families of woodwinds were represented by three or four players each, with English horn, bass clarinet, and contra bassoon consistently present. Several French composers added the alto saxophone on occasion. In the brass section more than four horns were often required, along with three trumpets, three trombones, and at least one tuba. Much new ground was broken in the use of percussion, with bells, cymbals, gongs, tambourine, xylophone, celesta, two harps, and four timpani incorporated. There were many innovators among late romantic orchestrators.

The Russians were original in their tendency to preserve individual colors. Among the most adept and creative, Tchaikovsky used a traditional ensemble, without bass clarinet or contra bassoon, but added percussion. The distinction between primary and secondary material was always clear, and scoring decisions seemed inevitably based on the musical idea. Rimsky-Korsakov was a master at exploiting unusual colors and very influential in this regard. His book, *Principles of Orchestration*, which was an important contribution to the field, contains many examples from his music.

Among the Germans, Wagner was the most imposing figure in this arena. His scoring for strings was extremely demanding, and he consistently mixed choirs of different types of instruments, unlike the Russians. Well known for excesses in all dimensions, Wagner is credited with the notation for the stopped

(+) horn technique. Mahler's economical yet dramatic style stood in contrast. Among the most explicit orchestrators regarding notation, Mahler wrote music that was also very different from Bruckner's, whose method was to use antiphonal choirs and score thickly. Brahms was not an innovative, adept orchestrator. His propensity for dense inner voices is inextricable from his compositional style. In general, Liszt patterned his orchestral style after Wagner's.

The French were original, scored cleanly, and avoided excess, traits shared by Saint-Saëns, Bizet, and Chabrier. Less fluent in this style was Franck, who had more in common with Bruckner. This may be due to the fact that they were both organists. In Italy opera reigned over instrumental music through the later romantic period. Verdi was a competent orchestrator who used the ensemble as an accompanist. Puccini exhibited complete control over the instruments and employed pitched percussion in an original manner. The Czech composer Dvořák is notable for clean, original scoring procedures that characteristically present the folk elements in his music. Sibelius, a composer from Finland who was unique in his extensive use of the low register for all instruments, deserves mention here also.

The master technician of the period was Richard Strauss. In his tone poems he made virtuosic demands on every instrument, sought extravagant colors, and was especially concerned with woodwind timbres and techniques. His music is extremely dramatic, with impassioned moods shifting as does the plot in a theatrical performance. In that instruments represent characters in poems or folktales, Strauss set an example for film scorers of the twentieth century.

TWENTIETH CENTURY

In the twentieth century a composer's individual musical style has greatly determined the use of orchestral resources. Although this is true of all periods, it is especially evident in contemporary music. The first unique style to emerge in the twentieth century was impressionism. Other schools, representing divergent orchestral styles, include the expressionist, the neoclassical, the neoromantic, and avant-garde experimentalist.

IMPRESSIONIST   The spirit and disposition of impressionists influenced their orchestral style. Woodwinds became equal in importance to strings, but in a subdued fashion. With blend and homogeneity the goals, the power of the brass was subverted by mutes and low dynamic levels. The colors of the pitched percussion instruments were exploited, as were special effects for strings. The overall sound was veiled, at times delicately punctuated, but quite transparent on the whole.

Debussy, whose *l'Après-midi d'un faune* was a significant contribution in 1894, stands at the forefront of the style. Romantic excesses were not appropriate for Debussy or Ravel, whose scores were filled with subtle shadings woven from thin, contrasting colors. The harp assumed an important role, and muted divisi strings were frequently called upon to play with tremolo techniques.

Ravel scored with exquisite restraint, almost in a classical manner. His ballet music, *Daphnis et Chloe* (1912), exhibits perhaps the highest craft in impressionistic orchestration. Ibert often scored in the impressionistic style, as did Milhaud and Poulenc at times. Influences were evident in the music of composers of the period outside of France as well. In Italy Respighi, in Spain Falla, in Brazil Villa-Lobos, and in America Griffes demonstrated their assimilation of the impressionistic ethos.

EXPRESSIONIST The orchestra became a vehicle for the dodecaphonic serial technique, the use of linear counterpoint was a common compositional device, an aural texture of pointillism was often preferred, and a propensity for mixing diverse timbres was evident. Extended techniques and the use of mutes became standard for the strings. Unconventional use of woodwinds and unusual combinations were sought after. The traditional role of the choir was shunned. Techniques such as flutter tonguing, glissandi, and muted forte passages were commonplace. The use of extreme registers for all instruments was typical. Percussion instruments were used carefully, and dry, high-pitched sounds were predominant.

Schoenberg's Five Pieces for Orchestra is a landmark work, displaying an application of his *klangfarbenmelodie* with extreme fragmentation of thematic material. Webern's scores are sparse, consisting of pointillistic leaps, lacking mass, and exploiting the use of silence. Berg's music is the most emotional of these three exponents of the style, and his opera score *Wozzeck* is a prime example of the expressionistic technique. As has always been the case, the orchestra was used to express the attitudes and philosophy of the composer.

NEOCLASSICAL Clarity was the purpose of neoclassical orchestration. It was accomplished in exemplary fashion in 1917 by Prokofiev in his Symphony No. 1. Stravinsky's orchestral style from the 1920s through the 1950s matched his neoclassical compositional style, and he is primarily responsible for the evolution of these techniques. His materials are controlled and contrapuntal, the parts soloistic, and the effect quite impersonal. Many twentieth-century composers, including Copland, Carter, Barber, and Piston employed neoclassical scoring techniques at times.

NEOROMANTIC There was a return to fullness of sound and a more passionate romantic spirit among many composers. Bartók and Hindemith, Shostakovich and Prokofiev, Britten and Vaughan Williams, Copland, Schuman, Harris, and Hanson can all be included in this group.

In general, large-scale forces were employed in all sections, particularly percussion. Not integrated with any particular compositional style, neoromantic scoring traits are evident in the works of such diverse composers as Honegger and Piston. There was a dichotomy, however, between the orchestrations in this style and those created by more avant-garde experimental composers.

AVANT-GARDE The experimentalists or avant-garde faction in the twentieth century have created works in order to expand the vocabulary and often the very precepts of an art form. Exoticism for its own sake has been applied to orchestration, with varied results. An early successful venture for the percussion ensemble was *Ionization*, written by Edgar Varèse in 1931. Penderecki and Ligeti both helped establish a new style with the use of sound masses, clusters, microtones, and innovative percussion. Numerous composers borrowed from non-European resources and developed music with Oriental and jazz elements. Electronic instruments and tape recordings are currently being combined with orchestral textures, as are acoustic sound sources previously not considered appropriate for the concert hall. Unusual seating arrangements and theatrical antics have been added to the business of music making. Aleatoric or improvisatory elements are becoming commonplace techniques, and their notation is having a significant impact on the appearance of modern scores.

ORCHESTRATION ANALYSIS

Just as it is possible to perform a harmonic or a structural analysis of a composition, one can perform an orchestration analysis. The following inquiries are useful to determine the composer's intent and purpose in constructing an orchestral score. Information about the use of instruments can be correlated with harmonic and structural analysis to provide a greater understanding of the music.

1. Identify all the instruments and their transpositions.

2. Determine the date of composition as it relates to the development of instruments, particularly valved brass.

3. Compare the orchestral style with other pieces from the period, taking into account standard instrumentation, grouping of choirs, and doublings.

4. Distinguish the primary lines or events from accompanimental parts, rhythmic patterns, coloration, and supporting harmony. Identify each instrument's role.

5. Consider the nature of the texture and the density of figure-ground relationships, and note the control of changes in texture.

6. Study the dynamic contours and levels, the weight or intensity of sections of the work compared to one another.

7. Identify the composer's principal sonorities, and see how the chords are spaced.

8. Explain special effects, score directions in any language, articulations, and other diacritical markings.

9. Comment on how the form of the piece is elucidated by varied instrumental colors and textural variations.

10. Name any unique, interesting features of the score that are peculiar to it and help differentiate it from other compositions.

SUGGESTED LISTENING

Mozart, Symphonies No. 35–41

Haydn, Symphonies No. 99–104

Beethoven, Symphonies No. 1–9

Schubert, Symphonies No. 8 (*Unfinished*) and 9 (*Great*)

Mendelssohn, Symphonies No. 3 (*Scottish*) and 4 (*Italian*) and *Midsummer Night's Dream* and *Hebrides* overtures

Schumann, Symphonies No. 1–4

C. M. von Weber, Overtures to *Der Freischütz,* and *Oberon*

Berlioz, *Symphonie Fantastique* and *Harold in Italy*

Dvořák, Symphonies No. 8 and 9 (*New World*) and Carnival Overture

Tchaikovsky, Symphonies No. 4, 5, and 6 (*Pathétique*), *Romeo and Juliet, Capriccio Italien,* and *Nutcracker Suite*

Brahms, Symphonies No. 1–4, *Academic Festival Overture, Variations on a Theme by Haydn,* and Piano Concerto No. 2

Bizet, *L'Arlésienne* Suite No. 1

Mahler, symphonies (all)

Bruckner, symphonies (all)

Franck, Symphony in D minor

Sibelius, symphonies (all)

Strauss, Tone poems (all), especially *Till Eulenspiegel, Don Juan, Tod und Verklärung, Ein Heldenleben, Don Quixote,* and *Also sprach Zarathustra*

Prokofiev, *Classical* Symphony and *Peter and the Wolf*

Debussy, *Prelude a l'Après-Midi, La Mer,* and *Nocturnes*

Rimsky-Korsakov, *Scheherazade* and *Capriccio Espagnol*

Stravinsky, *Firebird, Petrushka, Rite of Spring,* and symphonies (all)

Bartók, Concerto for Orchestra and The *Miraculous Mandarin*

Hindemith, *Mathis der Maler*

Shostakovich, Symphony No. 1

Mussorgsky/Ravel, *Pictures at an Exhibition*

Schoenberg, Five Pieces for Orchestra and Variations for Orchestra

Webern, 6 Pieces, Op. 5, and 5 Pieces, Op. 6

Berg, *Wozzeck*

Appendix A

Foreign Terminology

a cappella—unaccompanied voices
accelerando—gradually faster
ad libitum (ad lib.)—at will
al fine—to the end
alla breve—implies half note unit
allargando—slowing down, broadening
allegretto—slower than allegro
allegro—quick tempo
al segno—to the sign
alto—viola
anfang—beginning
arpa—harp
assai—very
a tempo—resume tempo
attacca—go ahead immediately
avec—with

battuta—strong beat
Becken—cymbals
bemolle—flat
ben—well
bien—very, well
Bratsche—viola
brio—spirit, vigor

caisse—drum
calando—softer and slower
campane—chimes
campanelli—orchestra bells

cantabile—singing style
carillon—orchestra bells
chitarra—guitar
cinelli—cymbals
coda—ending
col, coll, colla—with
con—with
cor—French horn
cor anglais—English horn
corda—string
corno—French horn
crescendo—increasing in loudness
crotales—antique cymbals
cuivré—brassy tone

da capo (D.C.)—from the beginning
Dämpfer—mute
decrescendo—decreasing in loudness
diesis—sharp
diminuendo—decreasing in loudness
divisi (div.)—divided, separate instruments
dolce—soft and sweet
Dur—major

einfach—unison
espressivo—expressive
etwas—some, somewhat

Fagott—bassoon

fermata—a pause or hold
forza—force
furioso—furious

gebunden—legato
gedämpft—muted
gehalten—sustained
Geige—violin
geteilt—divided, divisi
getragen—sustained
gewöhnlich—in the ordinary way
giocoso—playful
giusto—exact, proper
gran cassa—bass drum
Griffbrett—fingerboard

hautbois—oboe

istesso tempo—the same beat duration

Klavier—piano

langsam—slow
largamente—broadly
largo—slow and broad
legato—smooth
légerment—lightly
leggiero (legg.)—light
leggio—desk or stand
lento—slow
lustig—merry, gay

maestoso—majestic
mailloche—mallet or stick
marcato—marked
meno—less
mettez—put on (as in mute)
mezzo—half
mit—with
moines—less
Moll—minor
molto—very
morendo—dying away
mosso—motion

non—not
non troppo—not too much

obbligato—a countermelody
ohne—without
ossia—otherwise, alternate version
otez—remove (as in mute)
ottava (8va)—played an octave higher

Pauken—timpani
pesante—heavy, ponderous
piatti—cymbals
più—more
poco—little
ponticello—bridge
Posaune—trombone
pupitre—desk

quasi—almost, as if

rallentando (rall.)—slowing the tempo
risoluto—boldly, resolutely
ritenuto (rit.)—immediate slowing
Rohrenglocken—chimes
rubato—robbed, flexible tempo
ruhig—quiet

Saite—string
sans—without
Schellentrommel—tambourine
scherzando—playful
schmettern—brassy tone
schnell—quick
scordatura—other than normal tuning
secco—dry
segue—follows, continue or proceed
sempre—always
senza—without
simile—similar, continue
slentando—gradually slower
smorzando (smorz.)—dying away
sordino—a mute
sostenuto (sost.)—sustained

sotto—under
Steg—bridge of a string instrument
stretto—contracted, suddenly faster
stringendo (string.)—becoming faster
subito—suddenly
sur—on

tacet—is silent
tamburo militare—snare drum
tasto—fingerboard
tenuto (ten.)—hold to full value
timbales—timpani
tous—all
très—very
tromba—trumpet

troppo—too much
tutti—all together

umstimmen—change

vite—quickly
volti subito (v.s.)—turn page
   immediately
vorbereiten—prepare

wachsend—increasing in loudness

zeitmass—tempo
ziemlich—rather
zusammen—unison

Appendix B

Excerpts in Score

The musical examples in this appendix were selected because they show combinations of instruments in very effective ways. They also demonstrate stylistic traits of the composers who created them.

W. A. Mozart, Serenade, Eine kleine Nachtmusik, K. 525 (I, Allegro)

W. A. Mozart, Serenade, Eine kleine Nachtmusik, K. 525 (I, Allegro)

(continued)

W. A. Mozart, Serenade, Eine kleine Nachtmusik, K. 525 (I, Allegro), continued

W. A. Mozart, Serenade, Eine kleine Nachtmusik, K. 525 (I, Allegro)

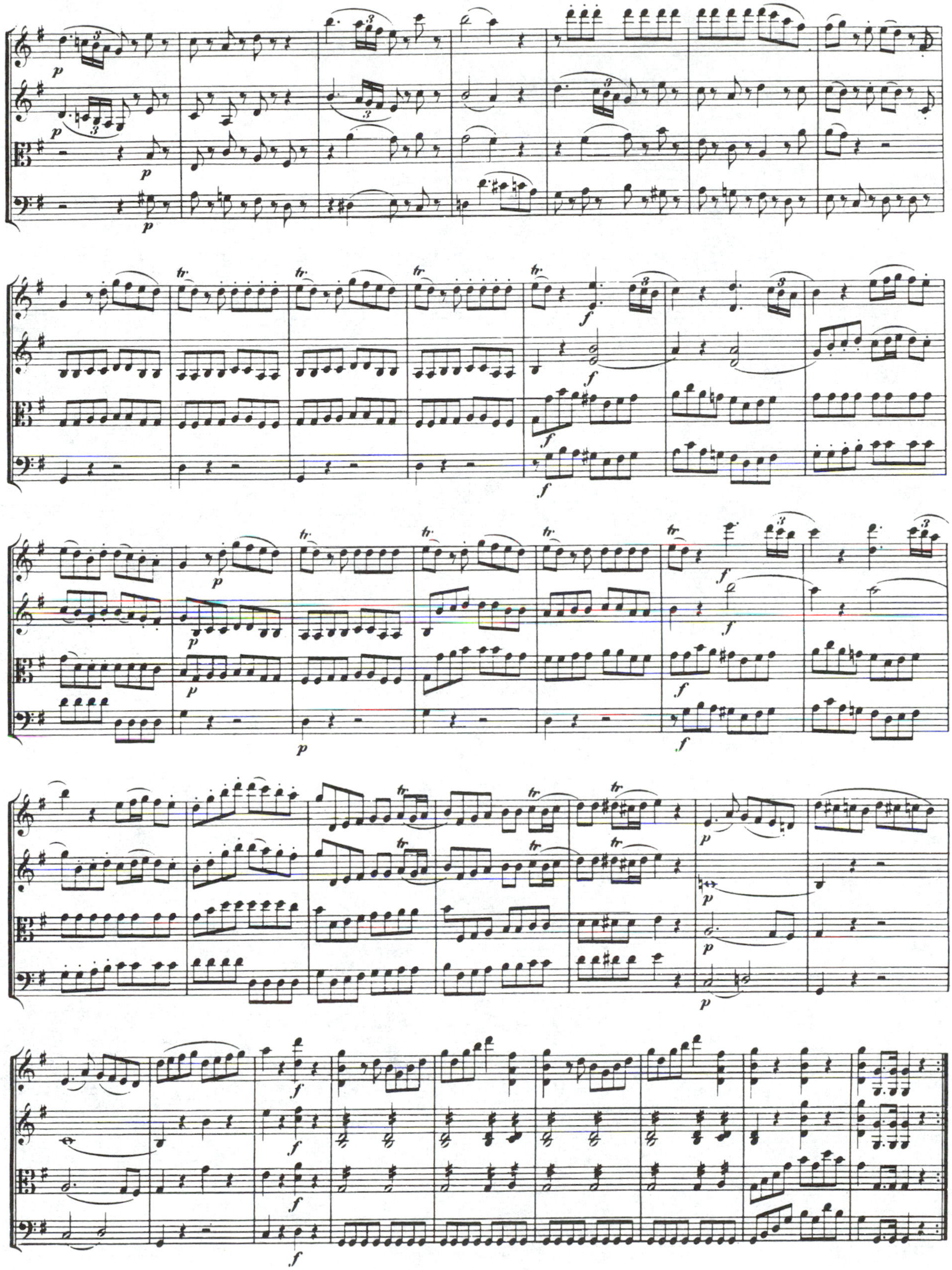

C. M. von Weber, Der Freischütz Overture (Measures 1–48)

C. M. von Weber, Der Freischütz Overture (Measures 184–207)

Felix Mendelssohn, Symphony No. 4 *(Italian)* *(III, Andante con moto moderato, last 65 measures)*

(continued)

Felix Mendelssohn, Symphony No. 4 (Italian) (III, Andante con moto moderato, last 65 measures), continued

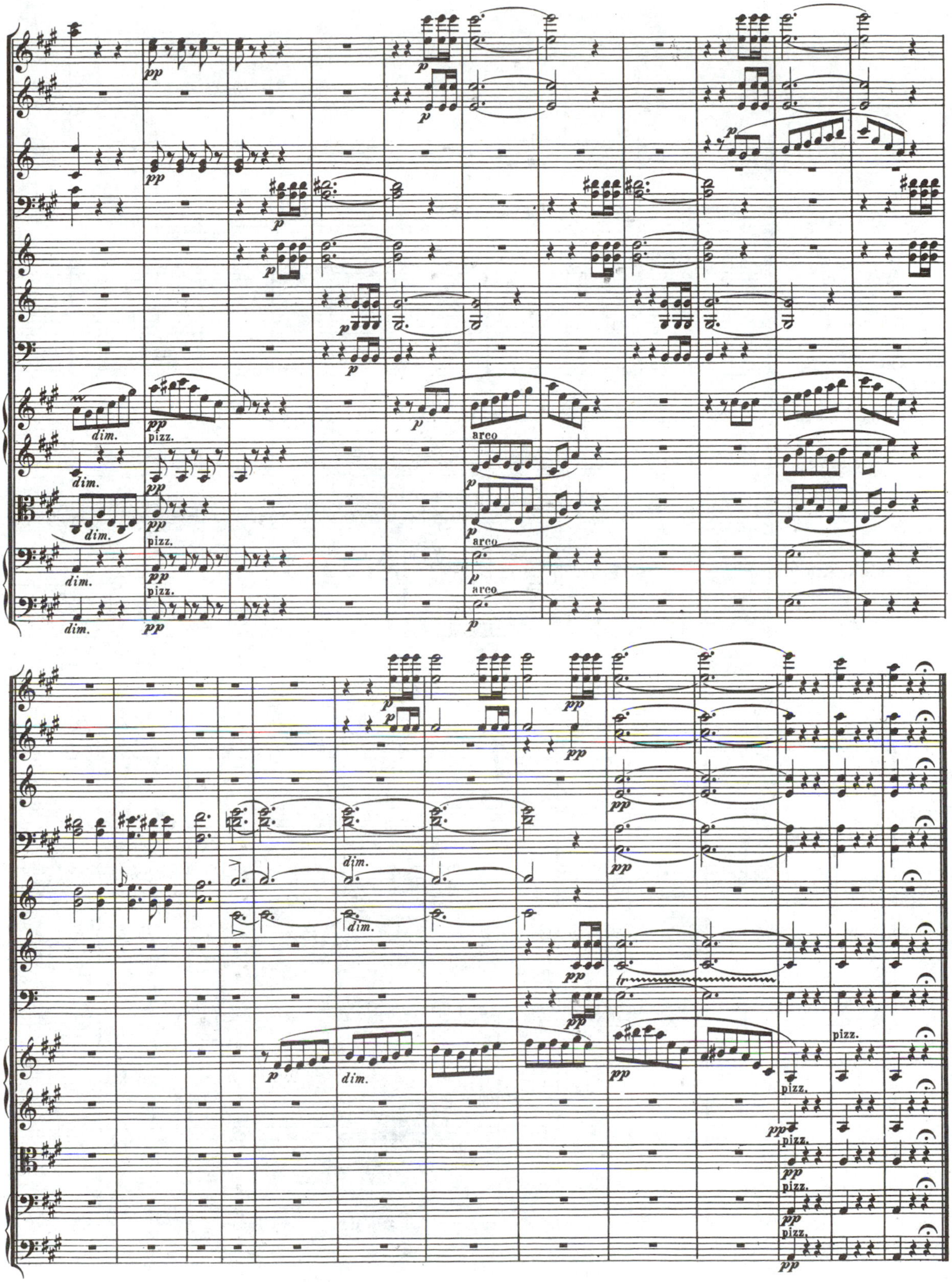
pp
p
dim.
pizz.
arco
tr

Ludwig van Beethoven, Symphony No. 5 (II, Andante con moto, measures 1–60)

Ludwig van Beethoven, Symphony No. 5 (II, Andante con moto, measures 1–60), continued

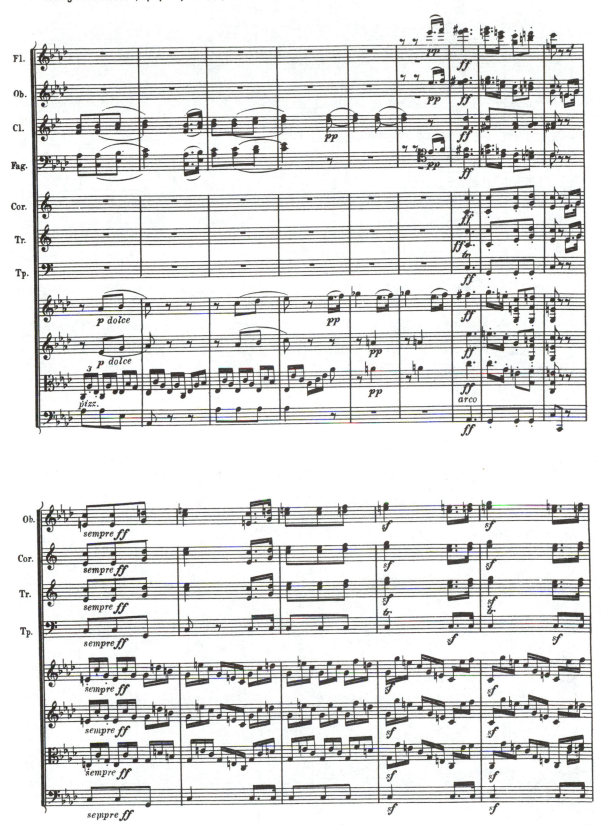

(continued)

(continued)

Ludwig van Beethoven, Symphony No. 5 (IV, Allegro, measures 1–46), continued

Ludwig van Beethoven, Symphony No. 5 (IV, Allegro, measures 1–46), continued

(continued)

BEETHOVEN, SYMPHONY NO. 5 127

(continued)

Ludwig van Beethoven, Symphony No. 5 (IV, Allegro, measures 1–46), continued

Georges Bizet, L'Arlésienne Suite No. 1 (II, Adagietto)

(continued)

(continued)

Peter Ilyitch Tchaikovsky, Symphony No. 6 (I, letter D to E)

Peter Ilyitch Tchaikovsky, Symphony No. 6 (I, letter D to E)

(continued)

Peter Ilyitch Tchaikovsky, Symphony No. 6 (I, letter T to the end)

(continued)

II

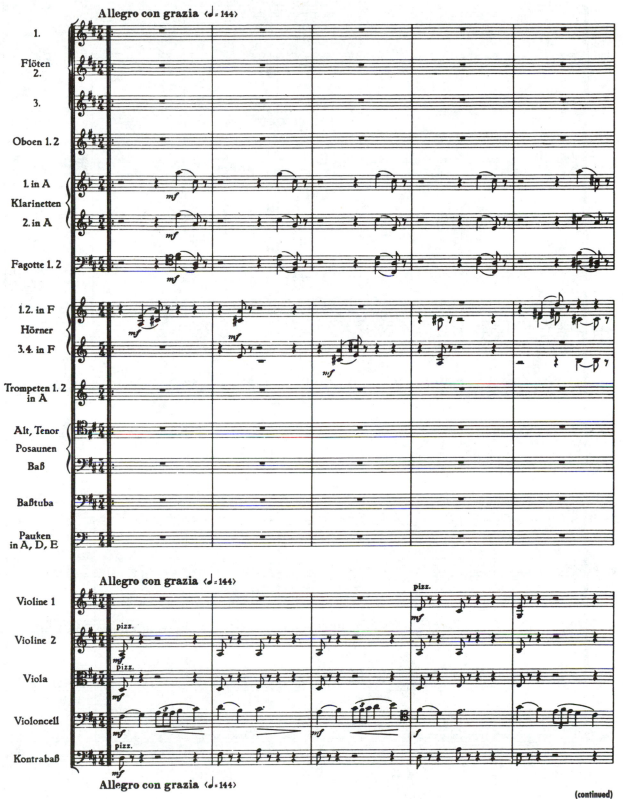

(continued)

(continued)

Peter Ilyitch Tchaikovsky, Symphony No. 6 (II, first 73 measures to letter F), continued

Peter Ilyitch Tchaikovsky, Symphony No. 6 (II, first 73 measures to letter F)

Peter Ilyitch Tchaikovsky, Symphony No. 6 (III, eight measures before letter U to letter W)

(continued)

Peter Ilyitch Tchaikovsky, Symphony No. 6 (III, eight measures before letter U to letter W)

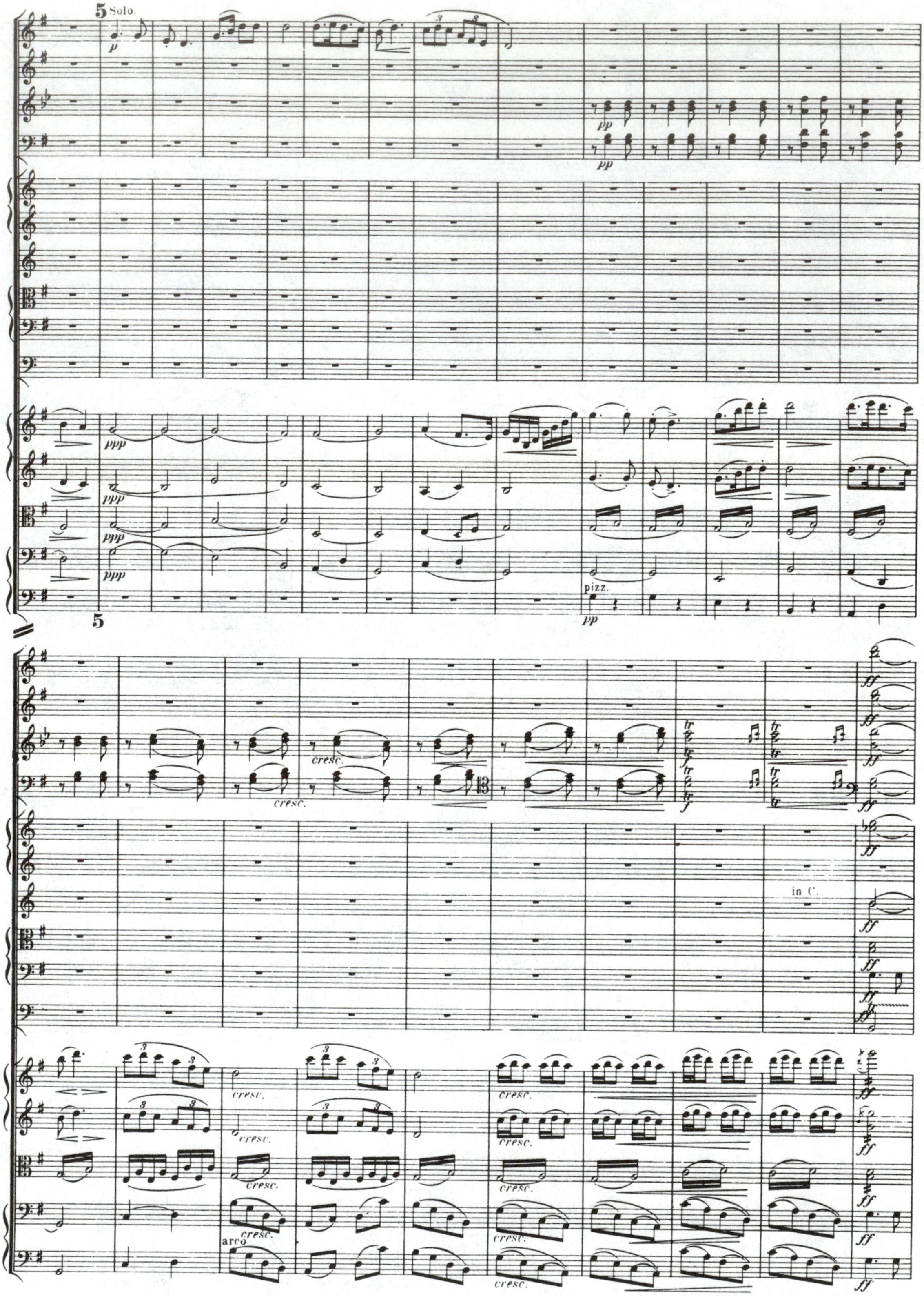
5 Solo.
p
pp
ppp
pizz.
5
cresc.
tr
f
ff
in C.
arco

Antonin Dvořák, Symphony No. 9 (New World) (I, measures 149–192)

(continued)

Antonin Dvořák, Symphony No. 9 *(New World)* (I, measures 149–192), continued

Antonin Dvořák, Symphony No. 9 (New World) (II, measures 21–63)

(continued)

Poco meno mosso.
a 2.
dim.
Poco meno mosso.
pizz.
pizz.
dim.
dim.
dim.
dim.
cresc.
dim.

Richard Strauss, Till Eulenspiegel (four measures before number 3 to one measure before number 5)

(continued)

kl. Fl.
3 Fl.
I.
II. III.
3 Ob.
I.
II. III.
engl. Horn.
Clar. (D)
2 Clar. (B)
3 Fag.
Contrafag.
4 Hörner (in F)
3 Tromp. (in F)
Viol.
I.
II.
Br.
Vcl.
C B.

Claude Debussy, La Mer (III, Dialogue du vent et de la mer, number 51 to eight measures after number 54)

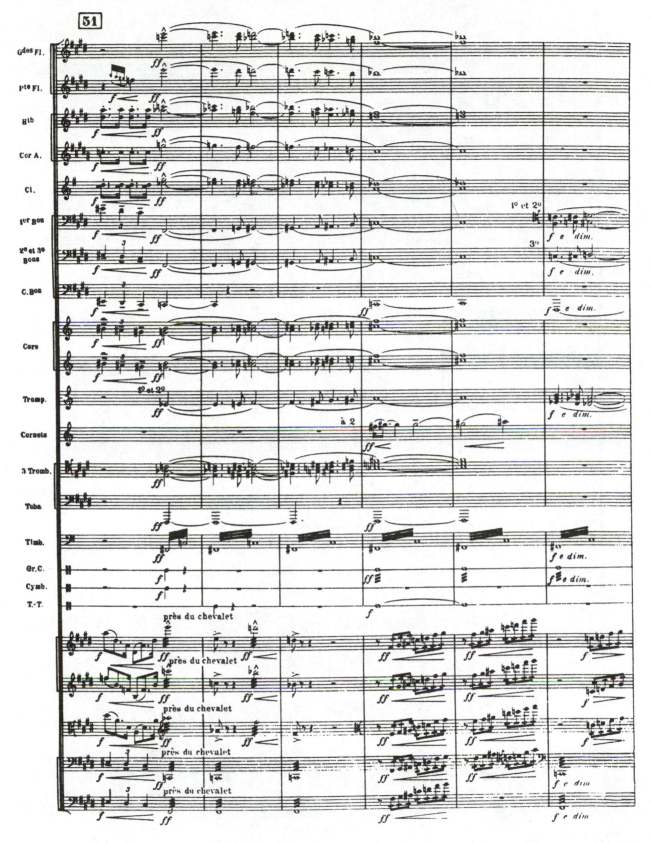

(continued)

Claude Debussy, La Mer (III, Dialogue du vent et de la mer, number 51 to eight measures after number 54), continued

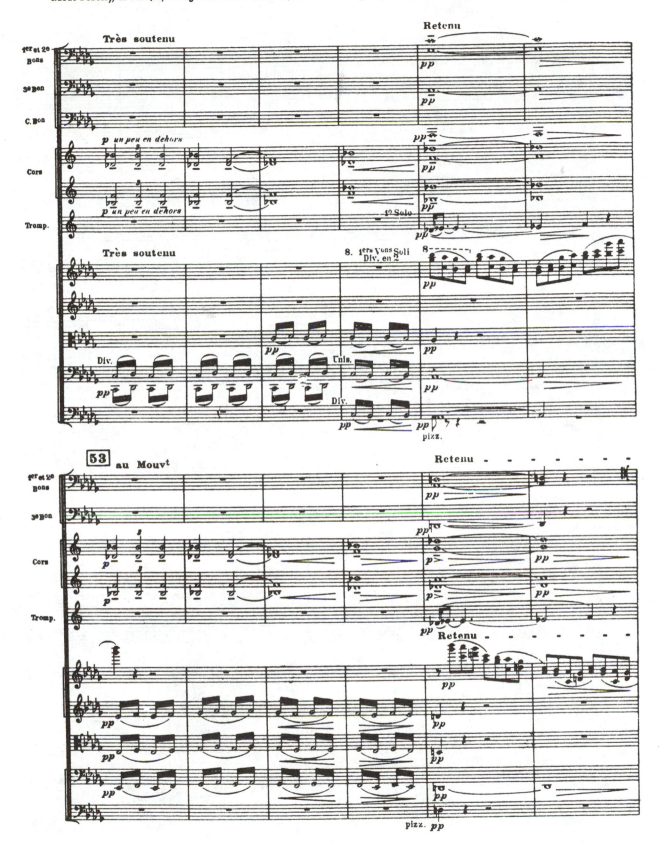

(continued)

Claude Debussy, La Mer (III, Dialogue du vent et de la mer, number 51 to eight measures after number 54), continued

Claude Debussy, La Mer (III, Dialogue du vent et de la mer, number 51 to eight measures after number 54)

Igor Stravinsky, *The Firebird (Number 149 to six measures after number 152)*

(continued)

Igor Stravinsky, *The Firebird* (Number 149 to six measures after number 152)

Appendix C

Scoring Projects

The projects in this appendix should be scored for six to eight available instruments and performed in class. Write the name of each instrument you use to the left of its staff on the score, and transpose it to the correct written key. Maintain the order found in an orchestral score, regardless of the combination: woodwinds, brass, percussion, and strings from top to bottom. Extract a part for each instrument to play, and conduct your arrangement. Do not use a keyboard instrument in these projects without your instructor's consent.

These are basically transcriptions from piano literature. Determine the best way to preserve the original musical content, not deviating radically from the original and keeping it in the same key if that is possible with the instruments available. After conducting your work, decide if the dynamics, articulations, and bowings you indicate achieve the desired results.

Following the five scoring projects for mixed chamber groups are five excerpts to transcribe for other larger ensembles.

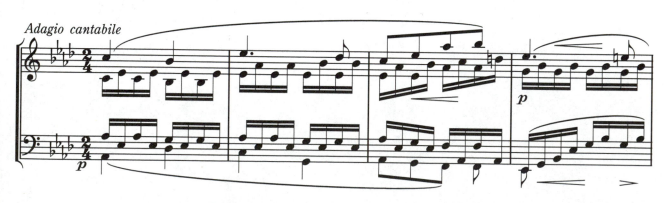

SCORING PROJECT 1. Beethoven, Sonata, Op. 13, II

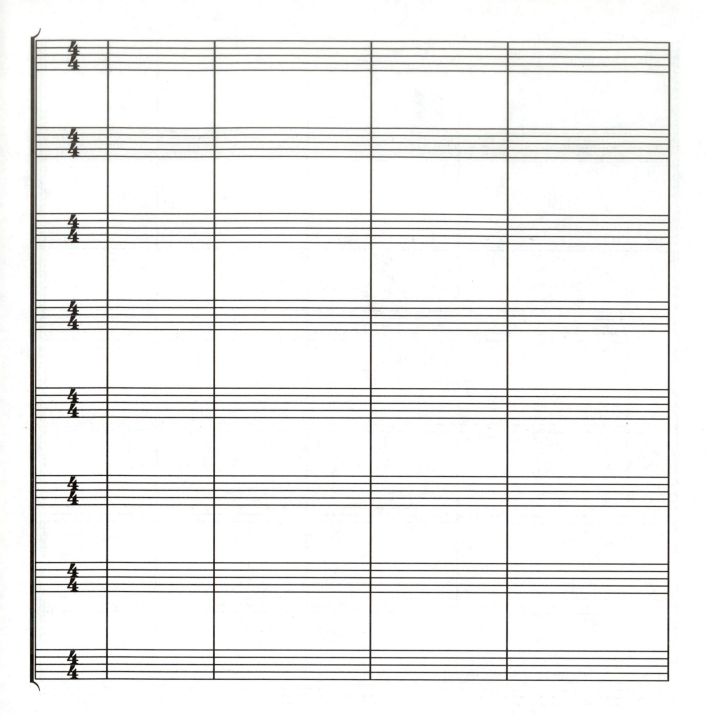

SCORING PROJECT 2. *R. Ehle, City Night Piece*

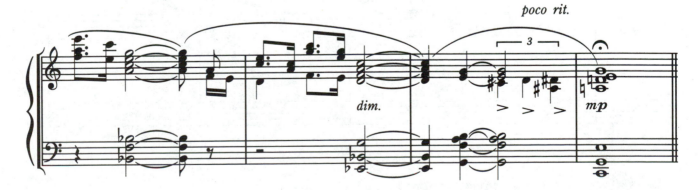

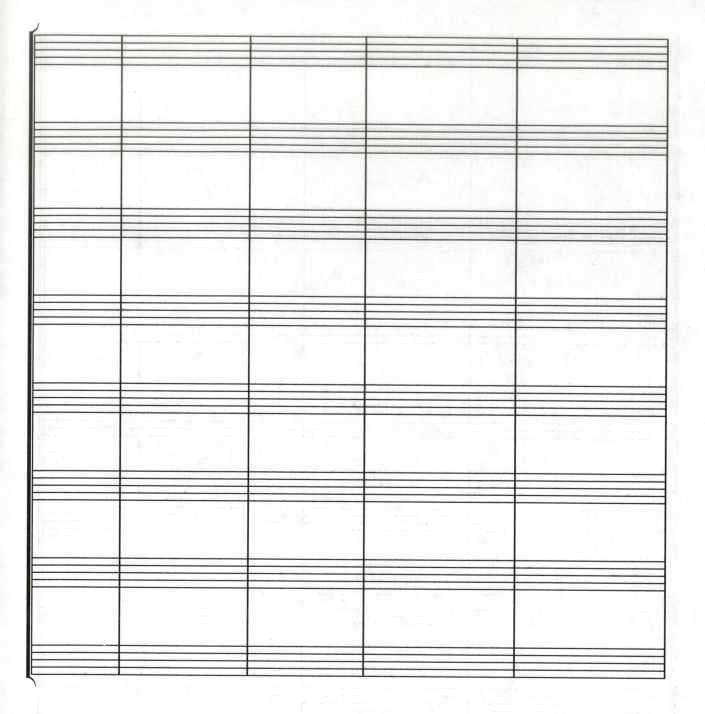

SCORING PROJECT 3. *Schumann, Traumerei*

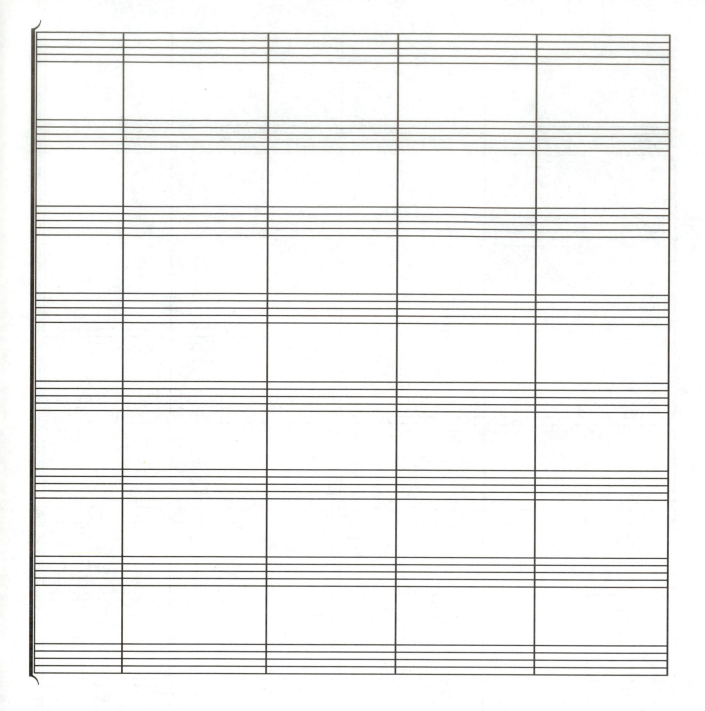

Andante cantabile

SCORING PROJECT 4.   *Chopin, Nocturne, Op. 15, No. 1*

SCORING PROJECT 5. *Debussy, Passapied*

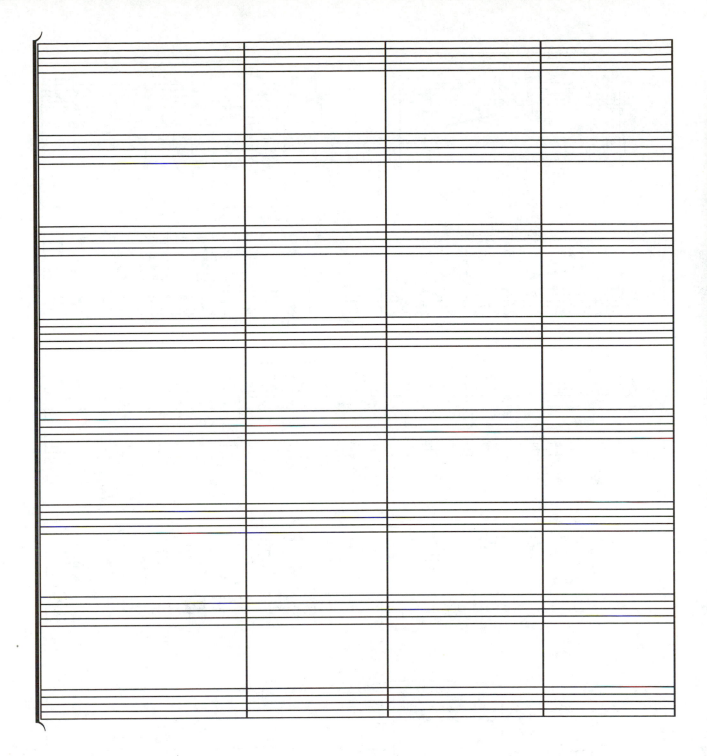

EXCERPT 1. *Brahms, Intermezzo, Op. 118, No. 2*

EXCERPT 1. *Brahms, Intermezzo, Op. 118, No. 2, continued*

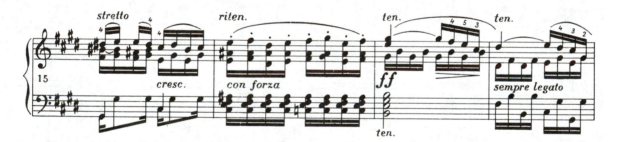

EXCERPT 2. *Chopin, Etude, Op. 10, No. 3*

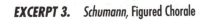

EXCERPT 3. *Schumann, Figured Chorale*

top
Clarinets oboes

8va tuba

8va t

EXCERPT 4. *J. S. Bach, Chorale, Wachet auf*

set up score
like 914

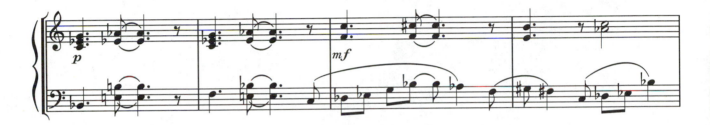

EXCERPT 5. *B. Hansen, Encore*

Annotated Bibliography

ADLER, SAMUEL. *The Study of Orchestration,* 2nd ed. New York: W. W. Norton, 1989. This very thorough reference or text treats both instrumentation and orchestration. It is a readable book, full of examples, including rarities as well as general information. The pedagogy assumes that listening to an example from the literature while examining the score is the preferred method of learning orchestration. Workbook and audio examples available.

BLATTER, ALFRED. *Instrumentation/Orchestration.* New York: Macmillan, 1980. This carefully written work is especially good for modern techniques and percussion devices. Among the most current references, this is a high-quality text.

BURTON, STEPHEN DOUGLAS. *Orchestration.* Englewood Cliffs, NJ: Prentice-Hall, 1982. This is a good source for commonsense information on the use of orchestral instruments.

KENNAN, KENT. *The Technique of Orchestration,* 4th ed. Englewood Cliffs, NJ: Prentice-Hall, 1990. This text, along with the workbook and audio recordings, takes a practical approach, with many references to the literature included in assignments and suggested listening.

RECENT TEXTS AND REFERENCES

BERLIOZ, HECTOR. *Treatise on Orchestration,* rev. R. Strauss, trans. Theodore Front. New York: E. F. Kalmus, 1948.

FORSYTH, CECIL. *Orchestration.* London: MacMillan, 1942.

McKAY, GARDNER. *Creative Orchestration.* Boston: Allyn & Bacon, 1963.

PISTON, WALTER. *Orchestration.* New York: W. W. Norton, 1955.

RIMSKY-KORSAKOV, NICOLAI. *Principles of Orchestration,* trans. Edward Agate. New York: Dover, 1953.

OLDER BOOKS ON ORCHESTRATION

BOOKS ON HISTORY AND DEVELOPMENT

CARSE, ADAM. *The History of Orchestration.* New York: E. P. Dutton, 1925.

PEYSER, JOAN, ed. *The Orchestra: Origins and Transformations.* New York: Charles Scribner's Sons, 1986.
This is a valuable collection of signed articles.

READ, GARDNER. *Style and Orchestration.* New York: Schirmer Books, 1979.
This unique book historically traces the development of orchestral styles with a generous number of musical examples. See also Read's *Thesaurus of Orchestral Devices* and *Contemporary Instrumental Techniques.*

GENERAL INFORMATION AND BOOKS ON INSTRUMENTS

BAINES, ANTHONY. *Woodwind Instruments and Their History.* New York: W. W. Norton, 1962.

BRINDLE, REGINALD SMITH. *Contemporary Percussion.* London: Oxford University Press, 1970.

DEL MAR, NORMAN. *Anatomy of the Orchestra.* Boston: Faber and Faber, 1981.

MARCUSE, SIBYL. *Musical Instruments: A Comprehensive Dictionary.* New York: W. W. Norton, 1975.

REED, OWEN, AND LEACH, JOEL. *Scoring for Percussion.* Englewood Cliffs, NJ: Prentice-Hall, 1969. Out of print.

SADIE, STANLEY, ed. *The New Grove Dictionary of Musical Instruments.* New York: Grove's Dictionaries of Music, 1984.

Subject Index

Music Index